CORONERS AND JUSTICE ACT 2009

EXPLANATORY NOTES

INTRODUCTION

1.   These explanatory notes relate to the Coroners and Justice Act 2009 which received Royal Assent on 12 November 2009. They have been prepared by the Ministry of Justice in order to assist the reader in understanding the Act. They do not form part of the Act and have not been endorsed by Parliament.

2.   The notes need to be read in conjunction with the Act. They are not, and are not meant to be, a comprehensive description of the Act. So where a section or part of a section does not seem to require any explanation or comment, none is given.

3.   A glossary of abbreviations and terms used in these explanatory notes is contained in Annex A to these notes.

SUMMARY

4.   The Act is divided into nine Parts.

5.   Part 1 reforms the law in relation to coroners and to the certification and registration of deaths. It replaces the existing framework for the investigation of certain deaths by coroners in the Coroners Act 1988 (the 1988 Act); that Act was a consolidation of existing coroner legislation, dating back to the early 1900s. In replacing the 1988 Act, this Part introduces a few new concepts. There will be a Chief Coroner to lead the coroners service, with powers to intervene in cases in specified circumstances, including presiding over an appeals process designed specifically for the coroner system. There will be a senior coroner for each coroner area (previously known as coroner districts) with the possibility of appointing area coroners and assistant coroners to assist the senior coroner for the area (in place of the existing deputy coroners and assistant deputy coroners). The 1988 Act was drafted almost exclusively in terms of "inquests" to refer to coroners' work. However, a significant amount of work goes on which does not lead to court proceedings and which was largely unrecognised in the 1988 Act. This work is reflected in the Act as it imposes a duty on a senior coroner to conduct an "investigation" into a death – it also reflects that a senior coroner may need to make preliminary inquiries to establish whether the death comes within his or her jurisdiction.

Chapter 1 of Part 1 makes provision for the conduct of investigations into deaths by senior coroners. Chapter 2 relates to the notification of deaths to the coroner and provides for the appointment of medical examiners and for the independent scrutiny and confirmation of medical certificates of the cause of death. Chapter 3 makes provision for coroner areas and for the appointment of senior, area and assistant coroners and provides for their funding. Chapter 4 makes provision in respect of investigations concerning treasure. Chapter 5 sets out the powers of senior coroners and offences relating to jurors, witnesses and evidence, and makes provision for payments to jurors, witnesses and others. Chapter 6 provides for the appointment of a Chief Coroner and Deputy Chief Coroners, provides for inspection of the coroners system and establishes a new appeals system in respect of certain decisions made by a senior coroner. The Chapter also enables the Chief Coroner, or a judge appointed by the Lord Chief Justice at the request of the Chief Coroner, to conduct an investigation into a person's death, instead of the senior coroner who would otherwise have jurisdiction. Chapter 7 contains other supplementary provisions, including provisions conferring powers on the Lord Chancellor to make "Coroners regulations" in respect of coroners' investigations and for "Coroners rules" in respect of coroners' inquests to be made by the Lord Chief Justice or his or her nominee. This chapter also provides for the abolition of the office of coroner of the Queen's household. Finally it provides for public funding for advocacy at certain inquests.

6.   Part 2 contains amendments to the criminal law. Chapter 1 amends the law in respect of the partial defences to murder and the offence and defence of infanticide, and simplifies and modernises the law on assisting or encouraging suicide. Chapter 2 creates a new offence of possession of prohibited images of children. Chapter 3 amends the law in respect of the offences of genocide, war crimes and crimes against humanity, creates a new offence relating to slavery, servitude and forced or compulsory labour and makes provision about conspiracies to commit offences in other parts of the UK. It also abolishes the common law offences of sedition and seditious libel, defamatory libel and obscene libel.

7.   Part 3 contains provisions relating to criminal evidence, investigations and procedure. Chapter 1 contains provisions for investigation anonymity orders. Chapter 2 re-enacts the Criminal Evidence (Witness Anonymity) Act 2008 (CEWAA) with some modifications. Chapter 3 contains provision about measures taken in court proceedings for vulnerable and intimidated witnesses. Chapter 4 contains provision about the use of live links in criminal proceedings. Chapter 5 contains miscellaneous provisions including provision extending the Queen's evidence provisions in the Serious Organised Crime and Police Act 2005 (the 2005 Act) to witnesses in prosecutions by the Financial Services Authority (FSA) and the Department for Business, Innovation and Skills (BIS), and provisions about the grant of bail in cases where a defendant is charged with murder.

8.   Part 4 relates to sentencing. Chapter 1 establishes the Sentencing Council for England and Wales (replacing the Sentencing Guidelines Council (SGC) and the Sentencing Advisory Panel (SAP)) and makes provision about the Council's functions and the duties of courts to follow its guidelines. Chapter 2 contains other provisions relating to sentencing. These provide for extended driving bans for persons also given custodial sentences and amend the law relating to sentences for dangerous offenders.

9.   Part 5 contains some further criminal justice provisions. It makes amendments relating to the Commissioner for Victims and Witnesses established under the Domestic Violence, Crime and Victims Act 2004; enables criminal offences created by regulations (under section 2(2) of the European Communities Act 1972) implementing Directive 2006/123/EC on Services in the Internal Market (the Services Directive) and Directive 2000/31/EC on certain legal aspects of information society services, in particular electronic commerce, in the Internal Market (the E-Commerce Directive) to have penalties exceeding those permitted by the European Communities Act 1972; amends a range of criminal procedure legislation to take account of the European Union Framework Decision 2008/675/JHA regarding the treatment in the UK of criminal offences committed elsewhere; and makes provision about the retention of knives confiscated from persons entering court and tribunal buildings.

10.   Part 6 contains provisions about civil and criminal legal aid, including provision for pilot schemes in relation to civil legal aid, and provisions about the enforcement of contribution orders made in cases where criminal legal aid is granted. It also makes provision for determining whether a "damages-based agreement" between a lawyer and a client that relates to an employment matter is enforceable.

11.   Part 7 introduces a new civil scheme through which courts can order offenders to pay amounts in respect of assets or other benefits derived by them from the exploitation of accounts about their crimes, for example, by selling their memoirs, or receiving payments for public speaking or media interviews. The scheme is restricted to cases where the memoirs, etc. pertain to offences which are triable only on indictment.

12.   Part 8 makes a number of amendments to the Data Protection Act 1998 (the 1998 Act), including amendments extending the inspection and audit powers of the Information Commissioner.

13.   Part 9 sets out supplementary provisions about (amongst other things) orders and regulations, commencement, extent and repeals.

BACKGROUND

14.   The purpose of the Act is to establish more effective, transparent and responsive justice and coroner services for victims, witnesses, bereaved families and the wider public. It seeks to achieve this by:

- updating parts of the criminal law to improve its clarity, fairness and effectiveness;

- giving vulnerable and intimidated witnesses, including those in respect of gun and gang related violence, improved protection, from the early stages of the criminal justice process;

- introducing a more consistent and transparent sentencing framework;

- improving the service bereaved families receive from a reformed coroner system;

- giving those who are suddenly or unexpectedly bereaved opportunities to participate in coroners' investigations, including rights to information and access to a straightforward appeals system; and

- putting in place a unified system of death certification that includes independent scrutiny and confirmation of the causes of death given on death certificates.

15.   In addition, the Act will confer stronger inspection powers on the Information Commissioner to improve the way that personal data is held and used.

Part 1 - Coroners etc

16.   The legislative changes in the Act are part of an overall package of reform aimed at addressing the weaknesses in the previous coroner and death certification systems, identified in the reports of the *Fundamental Review of Death Certification and Investigation* and the *Shipman Inquiry*, both published in 2003 (http://www.archive2.official-documents.co.uk/document/cm58/5831/5831.pdf and http://www.the-shipman-inquiry.org.uk/thirdreport.asp, respectively).

17.   A draft Coroners Bill was published in June 2006 (http://www.justice.gov.uk/docs/coroners_draft.pdf) and the public consultation on it ran until September 2006. This consultation took a number of different forms, including inviting written representations – more than 150 responses were received from a range of organisations and individuals. A summary report of the responses was published in February 2007 (http://www.dca.gov.uk/consult/coroners/cb684907b.pdf). A document setting out the changes to the proposals made in response to consultation was published in March 2008 (http://www.justice.gov.uk/docs/coroners-bill-changes.pdf).

18.   The draft Coroners Bill was subject to pre-legislative scrutiny by the then Constitutional Affairs Select Committee (CASC – now the Justice Committee). CASC's report on the draft Bill was published in August 2006 (http://www.publications.parliament.uk/pa/cm200506/cmselect/cmconst/902/902i. pdf). The Government responded to the CASC report in November 2006 (http://www.official-documents.gov.uk/document/cm69/6943/6943.pdf).

19.   In 2008, a consultation paper on the introduction of a statutory duty for medical practitioners to report deaths to coroners was published (http://www.justice.gov.uk/docs/cp1207.pdf). The Government decided that the statutory duty to report would be placed on registered medical practitioners only, and a draft list of the type of death to be reported was included in the response document (http://www.justice.gov.uk/docs/cp1207-response.pdf).

20.   A further consultation was carried out in April 2008 regarding sensitive reporting in coroner's courts (http://www.justice.gov.uk/docs/sensitive-reporting-coroners.pdf). The Government concluded that the Press Complaints Commission Code would not be amended and that instead consideration would be given to finding ways of drawing the Code to the attention of the bereaved families. The response to the consultation was published on 14 January 2009 (http://www.justice.gov.uk/docs/sensitive-reporting-coroners-courts.pdf).

21.   A consultation was carried out on a draft Charter for bereaved people who come into contact with the coroner service in June 2008 (http://www.justice.gov.uk/docs/draft-charter-bereaved.pdf). The consultation resulted in the Charter being revised, and the revised draft Charter was published on 14 January 2009 (http://www.justice.gov.uk/docs/charter-bereaved.pdf).

22.   A consultation on *Improving the Process of Death Certification* was published by the Department of Health in July 2007 (http://www.dh.gov.uk/en/Consultations/Closedconsultations/DH_076971). The public consultation ran until October 2007 and a summary of responses was published in May 2008 (http://www.dh.gov.uk/en/Consultations/Responsestoconsultations/DH_084949). The Department of Health received 157 written responses to the consultation and additional feedback through meetings with national stakeholder organisations and with councillors and representatives from local communities.

23.   The majority of respondents and participants in the consultative meetings recognised and acknowledged the problems with the previous process of death certification described in the consultation paper and supported the proposed improvements. The main concerns raised by respondents and participants were that the new scrutiny process should not cause significant delays to funerals and that medical examiners should be able to carry out their duties with the necessary degree of independence from the NHS and other public authorities. These two concerns have been critical factors in designing the improved process and will remain so in development of regulations and guidance.

Part 2 - Criminal offences

24.   On 28 October 2004 the Home Secretary announced (Hansard cols 1579-1580) that the Home Office, the Department for Constitutional Affairs and the Attorney General's Office would jointly review the law on homicide, with the first stage of the review being undertaken by the Law Commission and the second stage by the Government. In November 2006, the Law Commission published a report *Murder, Manslaughter and Infanticide* (available   at   http://www.lawcom. gov.uk/docs/lc304.pdf) – this completed the first phase of the review. On 12 December 2007 the Ministry of Justice announced (Hansard col. 43WS) the second stage of the review, stating that having considered the Law Commission's recommendations carefully the Government had decided to proceed on a step-by-step basis, looking first at the recommendations relating to:

- reformed partial defences to murder of provocation and diminished responsibility;

- the law on complicity in relation to homicide; and

- infanticide.

25.   In July 2008, the Government published a consultation paper *Murder, Manslaughter and Infanticide: proposals for reform of the law* including draft clauses (available at http://www.justice.gov.uk/publications/cp1908.htm). The Government received 74 responses to the consultation as well as running a number of stakeholder workshops and one-to-one meetings with key stakeholders. Having considered the responses to this consultation the Government decided to proceed with reforms to the partial defences to murder of provocation and diminished responsibility and reform of the law on infanticide. The strong message from the consultation was that complicity in relation to homicide should be reviewed in the context of the wider law on complicity, and the Government accepts that there are significant benefits to this approach. The summary of responses and a statement of the Government's position was published on 14 January 2009 (http://www.justice.gov.uk/publications/consultations-with-response.htm).

26.   Child psychologist Tanya Byron's report *Safer Children in a Digital World* published in March 2008 (http://www.dcsf.gov.uk/byronreview/) identified websites promoting suicide as an area where there is some confusion about the application of the law to on-line activity. It recommended that the law on harmful and inappropriate material (including suicide websites) should be investigated to see if it could usefully be clarified.

27.   Following such a review, the Government announced by way of a written Ministerial Statement on 17 September 2008 (Hansard col. 142WS) that it intended to simplify the law on assisting suicide to increase public understanding and reassure people that it applies as much on the internet as it does off-line.

28.   In reviewing the law, the Government took account of the Law Commission proposals in its report *Inchoate liability for assisting and encouraging crime* published in July 2006 (http://www.lawcom.gov.uk/docs/lc300.pdf) that the language of section 2 of the Suicide Act 1961 should be updated.

29.   In April 2007, the Government issued a *Consultation Paper on the Possession of non-photographic visual depictions of child sexual abuse*. A summary of responses was published in May 2008 (http://www.justice.gov.uk/publications/non-photographic-depictions.htm).

Part 3 - Criminal evidence, investigations and procedure

30.   On 18 June 2008 the House of Lords gave judgment in *R v Davies* [2008] UKHL 36. The case concerned the use of anonymous witnesses and the judgment cast doubt on what the common law had been thought to allow. The Government introduced the Bill that became the Criminal Evidence (Witness Anonymity) Act 2008 and it received Royal Assent on 21 July 2008. The Act makes provision about evidence given by anonymous witnesses. During the passage of the Bill, it was amended so as to provide for the expiry of the power to make witness anonymity orders on 31 December 2009, subject to being extended by order. This amendment became section 14 of the Act. The Justice Secretary undertook to review the provisions of the Act and legislate anew (Hansard col. 516; 26 June 2008). Chapter 2 of Part 3 of this Act replaces sections 1 to 9 of the CEWAA.

31.   In June 2007, the Government published *Improving the criminal trial process for young witnesses: a consultation paper* The Government response to the consultation was published   in   February   2009   (http://www.justice.gov.uk/ publications/young-witness-consultation.htm) The proposals in this consultation paper form the basis of the proposed changes in sections 98 to 103 to the existing provision about the special measures a court may order so as to help young witnesses give evidence.

32.   In the Policing Green Paper *From the neighbourhood to the national: Policing our communities together*, published in July 2008 (http://police.homeoffice.gov.uk/ police-reform/policegp/), the Government announced that it intended to remove a defendant's consent as to whether or not to attend a virtual court, where the participants are in a different location but are joined by live video link. Sections 106 to 110 give effect to this proposal.

33.   The law on admissibility of hearsay and out of court statements was comprehensively reviewed by the Law Commission in 2007 (*Evidence in criminal proceedings: hearsay and related topics*, published in July 2007, http://www.lawcom.gov.uk/docs/lc245.pdf). The law of evidence was also considered by Sir Robin Auld in *Review of the Criminal Courts of England and Wales* (2001) (http://www.criminal-courts-review.org.uk/). Both recommended that the law on hearsay should be simplified and that as much relevant evidence as is available should be able to be heard and considered. These recommendations were taken forward   in   the   White   Paper   *Justice   for   all*   published   in   July   2002 (http://www.cjsonline.gov.uk/downloads/application/pdf/CJS%20White%20Paper%20-%20Justice%20For%20All.pdf).

34.   A limited exception to the hearsay rule at common law had developed in relation to sexual offences. Where a complainant gave evidence, it was possible for the court to hear evidence as to the original complaint made by the victim provided the complaint was made spontaneously and at the first reasonable opportunity. The Law Commission recommended that evidence of recent complaint should not be limited to sexual offences. The Law Commission recommendations on recent complaint and other circumstances where previous consistent statements of witnesses are admissible led to section 120 of the Criminal Justice Act 2003 (the 2003 Act). Section 120 made a previous complaint by a victim of an alleged offence admissible subject to certain requirements, including a requirement that it was made as soon as could reasonably be expected after the conduct in question. Section 120 applies to all offences and is not limited to sexual offences.

35.   The Consultation Paper *Convicting Rapists and Protecting Victims – Justice for Victims of Rape* (Spring 2006) sought views on whether the law on previous complaints as set out in section 120 of the 2003 Act should be amended (http://www.cjsonline.org/downloads/application/pdf/Rape_consultation.pdf). In particular, it asked whether the requirement for a previous complaint to have been made "as soon as could reasonably be expected after the conduct in question" should be removed. There is evidence that in cases of rape and other serious sexual offences, victims often delay telling anyone of the offence because of feelings of shame, degradation and humiliation.

36.   The Government concluded in its *Convicting Rapists and Protecting Victims – Justice for Victims of Rape: Response to Consultation* (November 2007, http://www.cjsonline.gov.uk/downloads/application/pdf/Response%20to%20rape%20consultation.pdf) that the requirement for a previous complaint to have been made "as soon as could reasonably be expected after the conduct in question" should be removed and that this change should affect all offences. Making a general change is consistent with the provision as it currently stands (section 120(7) of the 2003 Act does not distinguish between types of offences) and reflects the fact there are other offences, such as those arising from domestic violence, where factors similar to those applying to sexual offences may cause victims to delay telling anyone about the offence.

37.   On 17 June 2008, the Government published a consultation paper *Bail and Murder*.The Government response to the consultation was published in February 2009 (http://www.justice.gov.uk/publications/cp1108.htm).

Part 4 – Sentencing

38.   The Sentencing Commission Working Group was set up by the Lord Chancellor and Lord Chief Justice in response to Lord Carter's review of the use of custody *Securing the Future*, December 2007. This review recommended that the Government "should establish a working group to consider the advantages, disadvantages and feasibility of a structured sentencing framework and permanent Sentencing Commission".

39.   The Working Group was chaired by Lord Justice Gage and made up of 15 members including lawyers, academics, judges, criminal justice professionals and others with experience in the field. The Working Group issued a consultation document A structured sentencing framework and Sentencing Commission on 31 March 2008 (http://www.judiciary.gov.uk/publications_media/general/sentencing_ consultation310308.htm).

40.   In its report, published on 10 July 2008, the Working Group recommended an evolutionary approach building on the existing processes for issuing guidelines and merging the Sentencing Advisory Panel (SAP) and Sentencing Guidelines Council (SGC) into one body (http://www.justice.gov.uk/publications/sentencing-commission.htm). Chapter 1 of Part 4 implements the unanimous and the majority recommendations of the report.

Part 5 - Miscellaneous criminal justice provisions

41.   Section 143 makes provision about the implementation of the E-Commerce Directive and the Services Directive.

42.   The Services Directive was adopted in December 2006 (http://eur-lex.europa.eu/LexUriServ/LexUriServ.do?uri=OJ:L:2006:376:0036:0068:EN:PDF).   The Directive seeks to facilitate the provision of services in the internal market ensuring the freedom of establishment and the freedom to provide services. Member States must implement the Directive by 28 December 2009.

43.   Chapter VI of the Directive ("Administrative Cooperation") enables greater cooperation between regulatory agencies ("competent authorities") across the European Union, so that they communicate more effectively with each other in the supervision of service providers.

44.   Article 30 of Chapter VI relates to situations where service providers operate in other member States on a temporary basis (that is where they are not established in that member State). Article 30(2) requires member States to ensure that their competent authorities do not refrain from taking action against service providers established in their territory on the grounds that the service has been provided or caused damage in a different member State.

45.   The Government published a consultation document on the implementation of the Services Directive in November 2007 (http://www.berr.gov.uk/files/file42207.pdf).   The Government Response to the consultation was published in June 2008 (http://www.berr.gov.uk/files/file46592.pdf).

46.   The E-Commerce Directive was implemented generically in the UK in 2002 by the Electronic Commerce (EC Directive) Regulations 2002 (SI 2002/33). The E-Commerce Directive seeks to contribute to the proper functioning of the internal market in the field of electronic commerce by ensuring the free movement of information society services ("ISS") between the member States.

47.   Article 3 of the E-Commerce Directive ("Internal Market") requires member States to regulate ISS in accordance with the country of origin rules. Article 3(1) requires each member State to ensure that the ISS provided by a service provider established on its territory comply with the national provisions applicable in the member State in question which fall within the coordinated field. "The coordinated field" covers all requirements in national law affecting the provision of ISS.

48.   Section 144 and Schedule 17 implement the Council Framework Decision (2008/675/JHA) of 24 July 2008 on taking account of convictions in the member States of the European Union in the course of new criminal proceedings (http://eur-lex.europa.eu/LexUriServ/LexUriServ.do?uri=OJ:L:2008:220:0032:0034:EN:PDF). Member States are required to implement the Framework Decision by 15 August 2010.

Part 7 - Criminal memoirs etc

49.   In November 2006, the Government published a consultation paper *Making sure that crime doesn't pay: proposals for a new measure to prevent convicted criminals profiting from published accounts of their crimes* (http://www.homeoffice.gov.uk/documents/cons-ensure-crime-doesnt-pay.pdf/). The summary of responses was published on 14 January 2009 (http://www.justice.gov.uk/publications/consultations-with-response.htm).

Part 8 - Data Protection Act 1998

50.   On 25 October 2007 the Prime Minister asked Dr. Mark Walport and Richard Thomas to conduct an independent review of the framework for the use of personal information in the public and private sectors. The Review's report was published on 11 July 2008 (http://www.justice.gov.uk/reviews/datasharing-intro.htm) and the Government response was published on 24 November 2008 (http://www.justice.gov.uk/publications/response-data-sharing-review.htm).

51.   The Government published a consultation paper on 16 July 2008, *The Information Commissioner's inspection powers and funding arrangements under the Data Protection Act 1998*. A summary of the responses to the paper and the Government's response were published on 24 November 2008 (http://www.justice.gov.uk/publications/cp1508.htm).

52.   In November 2007, the Prime Minister asked the Cabinet Secretary to lead a review of data handling procedures within Government. *Data Handling Procedures in Government: Final Report* was published by the Cabinet Office in June 2008 (http://www.cabinetoffice.gov.uk/reports/data_handling.aspx).

TERRITORIAL EXTENT

53.   In the main the Act's provisions extend to England and Wales only, but certain provisions also extend to Scotland or Northern Ireland or both (and there are also some bespoke Scottish or Northern Irish provisions mirroring equivalent provisions for England and Wales). In relation to Scotland, Wales and Northern Ireland, the Act addresses both devolved and non-devolved matters.

54.   The provisions of the Act relating to the following reserved matters extend to Scotland or are bespoke Scottish provisions:

- Amending the Fatal Accidents and Sudden Deaths Inquiry (Scotland) Act 1976 to facilitate investigations in Scotland into the deaths of service personnel killed abroad (section 50).

- Driving disqualification following conviction (section 137 and Schedule 16);

- Implementation of the E-Commerce Directive (section 143);

- Amendments to the 1998 Act (Part 8); and

- Amendments to (military) service law consequential upon other provisions in the Act.

55.   The Act contains provisions that trigger the Sewel Convention. The provisions relate to the implementation of the Services Directive (section 143) and criminal memoirs etc (Part 7). The Sewel Convention provides that Westminster will not normally legislate with regard to devolved matters in Scotland without the consent of the Scottish Parliament. The consent was given on 21 May 2009 (Official Report Col 17799 (http://www.scottish.parliament.uk/business/officialReports   /meetingsParliament/or-09/sor0521-02.htm#Col17799)).

56.   The provisions of the Act relating to the following excepted or reserved matters also extend to Northern Ireland or are bespoke Northern Irish provisions:

- The amendments to the Coroners Act (Northern Ireland) 1959 (the 1959 Act) made by section 49 and Schedule 11;

- Reform of the law on murder, infanticide and suicide (Chapter 1 of Part 2);

- The new offence of possession of non-photographic images of child sex abuse (Chapter 2 of Part 2);

- The new offence in England and Wales and Northern Ireland of holding someone in slavery and servitude, or requiring a person to perform forced or compulsory labour (section 71);

- The offence of conspiring in Northern Ireland to commit an offence in England and Wales or Scotland (section 72);

- Investigation anonymity orders and witness anonymity orders (Chapters 1 and 2 of Part 3);

- Extension of the Queen's evidence powers to the FSA (section 113);

- Driving disqualification following conviction (section 137 and Schedule 16);

- Enabling courts to pass an indeterminate sentence for public protection for certain terrorist offences (section 139);

- Implementation of the E-Commerce and Services Directives (section 143);

- Implementation of the Framework Decision on the taking account of convictions of member States in the course of new criminal proceedings (section 144 and Schedule 17);

- Provision for the seizure and retention of knives taken into court buildings (section 147);

- Criminal memoirs etc (Part 7);

- Amendments to the 1998 Act (Part 8); and

- Amendments to (military) service law consequential upon other provisions in the Act.

57.   In relation to Wales, the Act does not relate to devolved matters or confer functions on the Welsh Ministers, except for the following:

- Coroners – functions relating to the investigation of deaths by coroners are not devolved, but coroners are appointed and funded by local authorities. Under Schedule 2 to the Act, the Lord Chancellor will be required to consult the Welsh Ministers before making an order to specify the coroners areas for England and Wales or subsequently alter coroner area boundaries in Wales, and before he determines which one of a group of local authorities – within a coroner area – should act as the lead authority to liaise with coroners for various administrative purposes. Welsh Ministers will also be consulted on the appointment of a Medical Adviser to the Chief Coroner, who will give advice on medical issues across England and Wales to the Chief Coroner;

- Death certification – the Act places a duty on Local Health Boards to appoint medical examiners for Wales and section 19 gives the Welsh Ministers the power to make regulations about various matters relating to medical examiners;

- National Medical Examiner - Before appointing a person as National Medical Examiner under section 21, the Secretary of State must consult the Welsh Ministers.

- Sentencing – section 132 places a duty on the Sentencing Council to assess the impact on prison and probation resources of policy and legislative proposals, including proposals put forward by the Welsh Assembly Government, referred to the Council by the Lord Chancellor. Where an assessment relates to a proposal of the Welsh Ministers, the Act requires them to lay a copy of the Council's report of the assessment before the National Assembly for Wales.

58.   Section 181(9) makes provision in respect of section 79(3) of the International Criminal Court Act 2001 (the 2001 Act). That section permits Her Majesty to make provision by Order in Council to extend provisions of the 2001 Act to any of the Channel Islands, the Isle of Man or any colony. The effect of the amendment would be that the power in section 79(3) may be exercised in respect of the 2001 Act as amended by section 70.

THE ACT

COMMENTARY ON SECTIONS

Part 1 - Coroners etc

Chapter 1: Investigations into deaths

Section 1: Duty to investigate certain deaths
59.   This section sets out the circumstances when a senior coroner must investigate a death. It mirrors the requirements of section 8(1) of the 1988 Act, except that the requirement to investigate where the death is "sudden" or has occurred "in prison" (section 8(1)(c)) has been altered so that it applies to deaths where the deceased "died a violent or unnatural death," or "the cause of death is unknown" or "died while in custody or otherwise in state detention".

60.   The location of the body of the deceased will determine which senior coroner has a duty to investigate the death, as was the case under sections 5(1) and 8(1) of the 1988 Act. This is to ensure that more than one coroner does not initiate an investigation. Under the new system, senior coroners will, as now, be allocated to a geographical area, although later sections in Part 1 of the Act set out the circumstances when these boundary restrictions can be relaxed.

61.   *Subsection (2)* sets out the types of death that a senior coroner must investigate. A coroner must investigate a death that he or she suspects was violent or unnatural, where for example, the deceased might have been murdered or taken his or her own life, or if the cause of death is unknown. A coroner must also investigate a death, whatever the apparent cause, if it occurred in "custody or state detention" ("state detention" is defined in section 48(2)), such as while the deceased was detained in prison, in police custody or in an immigration

detention centre, or held under mental health legislation, irrespective of whether the detention was lawful or unlawful. The circumstances in which a coroner must investigate a death are broadly similar to those in section 8(1) of the 1988 Act. The requirement that a death be "sudden" has been removed. (Where other authorities have a statutory requirement to investigate particular deaths, such as the Health and Safety Executive or the Independent Police Complaints Commission, we anticipate that the coroner will await those authorities' reports before deciding how to proceed. This is apart from the commissioning of post-mortem examinations, where appropriate, and associated duties in relation to the body of the deceased person.)

62.   *Subsection (1)* is subject to section 2 (which makes provision for a senior coroner to request another senior coroner to conduct the investigation), section 3 (under which the Chief Coroner may direct that an investigation be conducted by a different senior coroner from the one who would otherwise be under a duty to conduct it), section 4 (which makes provision for an investigation to be discontinued) and Schedule 10 (which makes provision for persons other than the senior coroner in the area where the body is to conduct the investigation).

63.   A senior coroner's initial decision as to whether to conduct an investigation will be subject to appeal to the Chief Coroner under section 40.

64.   *Subsections (4)* to *(6)*, which correlate to section 15 of the 1988 Act, set out the arrangements for investigating deaths when the senior coroner thinks that a death has occurred which should be investigated but there is no body; and so the duty to investigate the death in subsection (1) does not apply. This includes circumstances such as where a body has been lost at, or swept away to, sea, or if someone is suspected to have lost their life in a fire and there are no remains, or if the deceased has already been cremated and information previously unavailable comes to light which the senior coroner believes should lead him or her to investigate.

65.   These subsections allow a senior coroner to report the details of such a death to the Chief Coroner, who may direct an investigation be held.

66.   Under the 1988 Act it was the Secretary of State who could direct a coroner to conduct an inquest in the absence of a body. In the reformed system, the Chief Coroner might also decide that no investigation is necessary. If the Chief Coroner decides that action should be taken, the senior coroner directed to carry out the investigation does not have to be the same coroner that reported the death although in most circumstances it is likely that it would be. An example of a reason the Chief Coroner might have for allocating the case to a different coroner is that it might be more convenient for the bereaved relatives for the investigation to take place in an alternative area.

67.   Provision is made in *subsection (7)* enabling a coroner to make whatever enquiries are thought to be necessary in order to help the coroner decide whether the duty under subsection (1) (to conduct an investigation into a death) or the power under subsection (4) (to report a death where there is no body) arises.

Section 2: Request for other coroner to conduct investigation

68.   This section gives the senior coroner the power to transfer responsibility for the investigation of a death to another coroner, where that coroner agrees. It is broadly similar to section 14 of the 1988 Act, which allowed a coroner in one district to ask a coroner of another district to assume jurisdiction to hold an inquest into the death.

69.   Under *subsection (2)*, a senior coroner who agrees to conduct an investigation on behalf of another coroner must carry out that investigation as soon as possible. No other coroner can conduct the investigation. The coroner who agrees to deal with the investigation will have powers to move the body, in order to ensure a more efficient inquiry. We anticipate that how costs will be apportioned in transferred cases will be dealt with in regulations under section 43.

70.   This section does not apply where the Chief Coroner directs another coroner to conduct an investigation under section 3.

71.   Examples of cases where the coroner may wish to ask another coroner to conduct the investigation include cases where the bereaved relatives and/or most of the witnesses in the case live in the other coroner's area; and cases where there is a major incident across more than one coroner area, and the Government believes that it is more efficient for only one coroner to lead the investigation and to be seen as the point of contact for bereaved people.

Section 3: Direction for other coroner to conduct investigation

72.   This section gives the Chief Coroner the power to direct a senior coroner who is not the coroner under a duty to investigate a death under section 1 to conduct an investigation. It is developed from section 14(2) of the 1988 Act. The Government intends that this provision will enable the Chief Coroner to respond effectively to an emergency situation, or to reallocate work between coroners in the event of backlogs of work building up in a particular area. Reallocations of this type should take account of the needs of bereaved relatives for both a prompt investigation and one that remains fairly local to them.

73.   Under *subsection (2)*, a coroner who is directed by the Chief Coroner to carry out an investigation must do so. No other coroner can conduct the investigation. The coroner directed to deal with the investigation will have powers to move the body, in order to ensure a more efficient inquiry. Again, we anticipate that how costs will be apportioned in transferred cases will be dealt with in regulations under section 43.

74.   The Chief Coroner may give more than one direction under section 3. For example, if the coroner who has been directed to conduct an investigation is unable to deal with it, the Chief Coroner may direct another coroner to investigate instead.

Section 4: Discontinuance where cause of death revealed by post-mortem examination

75.   This section allows a senior coroner to discontinue an investigation which was started because the cause of death was unknown. The coroner may discontinue such an investigation if a post-mortem examination under section 14 reveals the cause of death, and the coroner thinks that it is not necessary to continue the investigation; an inquest will not therefore be required. This may be because, for example, the death is shown to be due to natural causes and there are no other circumstances (such as state detention) associated with the death which would mean that the investigation needs to continue to an inquest. The coroner may not discontinue the investigation if he or she suspects the deceased died a violent or unnatural death, or died whilst in state detention. This is developed from section 19 of the 1988 Act.

76.   If a senior coroner discontinues an investigation under this section he or she is not permitted to go on to hold an inquest into the death or make any determination. The section includes a new requirement for the coroner to explain why an investigation has been discontinued if asked to do so. There is also provision for a fresh investigation to be conducted if, for example, new information comes to light.

Section 5: Matters to be ascertained

77.   This section sets out the purpose of a senior coroner's investigation.

78.   The two purposes of an investigation are: (1) to establish who the deceased was and how, when and where the deceased came by his or her death, and (2) to establish the details needed to register the death (such as the cause of death). These purposes were previously contained in rule 36(1) of the Coroners Rules 1984 (the 1984 Rules), and in section 11(5)(b) of the 1988 Act.

79.   *Subsection (2)* requires the scope of the investigation to be widened to include an investigation of the broad circumstances of the death, including events leading up to the death in question, where this wider investigation is necessary to ensure compliance with the European Convention on Human Rights (ECHR), in particular Article 2. Article 2 relates to the State's responsibility to ensure that its actions do not cause the death of its citizens. The Act does not define the precise circumstances where a coroner should conduct an Article 2 investigation. This will allow for flexibility in the future should case law determine that Article 2 inquests should extend to cover additional matters. Such information could, however, be contained in guidance issued by the Chief Coroner.

Section 6: Duty to hold inquest

80.   Section 6 provides that the coroner must conduct an inquest as part of the investigation unless he or she has had reason to discontinue it under section 4, following a post-mortem examination

81.   The 1988 Act is expressed in terms of a duty to "hold an inquest". This does not reflect the entirety of what coroners do. In 2008, some 235,000 deaths were reported to a coroner, and there were about 31,000 inquests. Under the Act, the inquest will form, when relevant, the final part of the investigation process. The Government does not anticipate that the number of inquests will increase or decrease significantly in a reformed system.

Section 7: Whether jury required
82.   This section sets out the circumstances in which a senior coroner is required to hold an inquest into a death with a jury. It also gives the coroner the power to decide to hold an inquest with a jury in any case where he or she thinks there is sufficient reason. It is modelled on section 8(3) of the 1988 Act.

83.   The general rule is that an inquest must be held without a jury. *Subsections (2)* and *(3)* set out the exceptions to this rule. A jury must be summoned where the deceased died while in custody or otherwise in state detention, and the death was violent or unnatural, or of unknown cause; where the death was as a result of an act or omission of a police officer or member of a service police force (defined in section 48) in the purported execution of their duties; or where the death was caused by an accident, poisoning or disease which must be reported to a government department or inspector. This includes, for example, certain deaths at work. Although a jury is not required in any other case the coroner will be able to summon one in any case where he or she believes there is sufficient reason for doing so.

84.   The Government will in secondary legislation make further, more detailed provision about the conduct of inquests (in the Coroners rules to be made under section 45).

85.   Under section 40 interested persons, as defined in section 47, will be able to appeal against a coroner's decision to summon a jury or not to do so in those cases where the senior coroner has discretion.

Section 8: Assembling a jury
86.   This section sets out the arrangements for summoning and swearing in a jury.

87.   *Subsection (1)* sets out the numbers of jurors for a coroner's jury. There must be no fewer than seven and not more than eleven people. This replicates the minimum and maximum number of jurors under section 8(2)(a) of the 1988 Act.

88.   The senior coroner calls people to attend for jury service by issuing a summons stating the time that they are needed and the place that they must attend *(subsection (2))*, as under the previous arrangements. At the outset the coroner will require jury members to swear they will make a true determination according to the evidence *(subsection (3))*.

89.   *Subsection (4)* makes qualifications for jury service at a coroner's inquest the same as for the Crown Court, the High Court and the county courts, in accordance with section 1 of the Juries Act 1974. This reproduces the requirements of section 9(1) of the 1988 Act.

90.   *Subsection (5)* enables the coroner to check that a juror meets the qualification requirements, in the same terms as section 9(4) of the 1988 Act.

Section 9: Determinations and findings by jury

91.   A jury will be initially directed by the senior coroner to reach a unanimous determination or finding. If the coroner thinks that they have deliberated for a reasonable time without reaching a unanimous verdict, under *subsection (2)*, he or she may accept a determination or finding on which the minority consists of no more than two persons. Also under *subsection (2)*, the jury spokesperson should announce publicly how many agreed. If the required number of jurors does not agree, under *subsection (3)* the coroner may discharge the jury and summon a completely new jury and the case will be heard again.

Section 10: Determinations and findings to be made

92.   This section explains what happens at the conclusion of the inquest. It sets out the possible outcomes and explains their effect.

93.   *Subsection (1)(a)* requires the senior coroner – or the jury, where there is one – to make a "determination" at the end of the inquest as to who the deceased was, and how, when, where the deceased came by his or her death. This is broadly equivalent to the requirements under section 11(3)(a) and (4)(a) of the 1988 Act and rule 36 of the 1984 Rules. In an investigation where Article 2 ECHR is engaged, the coroner must also include a determination, or direct a jury to include a determination, as to the circumstances of the death.

94.   *Subsection (1)(b)* also requires the coroner or jury to make a "finding" at the end of the inquest about the details required for registration of the death, as was required by section 11(3)(b) and (4)(b) of the 1988 Act. This will normally be, for example, a short finding such as accident or misadventure, suicide, industrial disease, natural causes, drug related or, where no clear cause has death has been established, the finding will be known as "open". Increasingly, coroners make use of "narrative" findings in which they sum up (usually in a few sentences) how the person came to die.

95.   *Subsection (2)* makes clear that a determination may not be worded in such a way as to appear to determine any question of criminal liability of any named person or to determine any question of civil liability.

Section 11 and Schedule 1: Duty or power to suspend or resume investigations

96.   This section gives effect to Schedule 1 which contains provisions on suspending and resuming investigations in various situations. Schedule 1 sets out when a senior coroner can or must suspend and resume investigations.

Paragraph 1: Suspension of investigation where certain criminal charges may be brought

97.   *Paragraph 1* of Schedule 1 contains provision for suspending the senior coroner's investigation in the event that it is likely that criminal proceedings will be brought in connection with the death. It is intended to avoid duplicate investigations. This is based on rules 26 and 27 of the 1984 Rules.

98.   This will mean firstly, under *Paragraphs 1(2)* and *1(3)* that the senior coroner will suspend an investigation if asked to do so by a prosecuting authority, including the Provost Marshal or the Director of Service Prosecutions in relation to service equivalents, because someone may be charged with a homicide or other offence directly involving or indirectly related to the death of the deceased.

99.   Secondly, under *paragraph 1(4)*, if the senior coroner has to suspend an investigation under paragraphs 1(2) or 1(3), the suspension must be for at least 28 days. The senior coroner has the power to extend (more than once if needed) the period of the suspension if asked to do so by the person who or authority which requested the original suspension (through *paragraph 1(5)*) or the Director of Service Prosecutions (in a paragraph 1(4) case).

100.   Finally, *paragraph 1(6)* defines "homicide offence","related offence" and the "service equivalent of a homicide offence" as used in this paragraph.

Paragraph 2: Suspension where certain criminal proceedings are brought
101.   *Paragraph 2* of Schedule 1 sets out the arrangements for suspension of the senior coroner's investigation when criminal proceedings have been brought in connection with the death. It is developed from section 16 of the 1988 Act.

102.   The effect of *paragraph 2(2)* is that a senior coroner must suspend an investigation into a death on becoming aware either that someone has appeared or been brought before a magistrates' court charged with a homicide offence involving the death of the deceased or that they have been charged on indictment in the Crown Court with such an offence. Similarly, under *paragraph 2(4)*, when a coroner becomes aware that someone has been charged with an offence related to the death under investigation (whether it is before the magistrates' court or the Crown Court), the senior coroner is also required to suspend the investigation. As set out in *paragraphs 2(3) and 2(5)*, these duties also apply to the service equivalents of such offences.

103.   The senior coroner need not suspend an investigation under paragraph 2(2), (3) or (4) where the prosecuting authority or the Director of Service Prosecutions (as the case may be) has no objection to the investigation continuing or where the senior coroner thinks that there is exceptional reason for not doing so *(paragraph 2(6))*.

104.   *Paragraph 2(7)* makes provision for investigations which had been suspended under paragraph 1, and which are then subsequently suspended under paragraph 2.

Paragraphs 3 and 4: Suspension pending inquiry under Inquiries Act 2005
105.   *Paragraph 3* of Schedule 1 sets out the circumstances in which a senior coroner's investigation must be suspended where there is an inquiry under the Inquiries Act 2005. It is based on section 17A of the 1988 Act.

106. *Paragraph 3(1)* requires the senior coroner to suspend an investigation into a death if requested to do so by the Lord Chancellor on the basis that there will be an inquiry under the Inquiries Act 2005 in which the cause of death is likely to be adequately investigated; that a senior judge has been appointed to chair such an inquiry; and that the Lord Chief Justice has approved (for the purposes of paragraph 3) that appointment. The senior coroner does not have to suspend an investigation if he or she thinks there are exceptional reasons for continuing with it (*paragraph 3(2)*). *Paragraph 3(3)* makes provision for investigations which are already suspended under paragraph 1.

107. *Paragraph 4* further provides that in situations where an investigation has been suspended on the basis that the cause of death is likely to be adequately investigated by an inquiry set up under the Inquiries Act 2005, the terms of reference of that inquiry must include the purposes set out in section 5(1) of this Act – that is who the deceased was and how, when and where the deceased came by his or her death (read with section 5(2) where necessary to comply with Convention rights). As noted above, all such inquiries will be chaired by a senior member of the judiciary – in this case, a High Court judge, a Court of Appeal judge or a Justice of the Supreme Court.

Paragraph 5: General power to suspend
108. *Paragraph 5* of Schedule 1 provides a general power for a senior coroner to suspend an investigation if he or she thinks that it would be appropriate to do so. This may be appropriate if another investigation is being conducted into the death, for example, by the Independent Police Complaints Commission, the Health and Safety Executive or an Accident Investigation Branch, or if an investigation is being conducted in another jurisdiction, for example, if the death occurred abroad.

Paragraph 6: Effect of suspension
109. Where an investigation is suspended under paragraphs 1, 2, 3 or 5, any inquest being held as part of that investigation must also be adjourned and if it is being held with a jury, the senior coroner may discharge the jury.

Paragraph 7: Resumption of investigation suspended under paragraph 1
110. If the senior coroner suspends an investigation because someone may be charged with an offence, the investigation must be resumed (subject to paragraphs 2(7)(d) and 3(3)(b)) once the relevant period has expired.

Paragraph 8: Resumption of investigation suspended under paragraph 2
111. *Paragraph 8* of Schedule 1 sets out the arrangements for resuming investigations suspended because certain criminal proceedings have been brought.

112. Under *paragraph 8(1)* the senior coroner can resume an investigation only if he or she thinks there is sufficient reason to do so.

113. *Paragraph 8(2)* ensures that the investigation cannot be resumed until the criminal proceedings which triggered the suspension have come to an end in the court of trial.

114.   This is qualified by *paragraph 8(3),* under which the investigation can be resumed, even if the criminal proceedings are continuing, providing the relevant prosecuting authority (as defined in *paragraph 8(4)*) has confirmed it has no objection.

115.   *Paragraph 8(5)* makes clear that the outcome of a coroner's investigation resumed under this paragraph must be consistent with the result of the criminal proceedings which triggered the suspension.

116.   It could be that the senior coroner resumes the investigation because the criminal investigation did not find all the facts that the senior coroner is required to find or because it did not meet ECHR Article 2 obligations, for example because the defendant pleaded guilty. Indeed the effect of section 6(1) of the Human Rights Act 1998 (HRA) is that the senior coroner, as a public authority, would be legally obliged to resume the investigation if this was necessary in order to secure compliance with Article 2.

Paragraph 9: Resumption of investigation suspended under paragraph 3
117.   *Paragraph 9* of Schedule 1 sets out the arrangements for resuming investigations suspended because of an inquiry. Under *paragraph 9(1)* the senior coroner can resume an investigation only if he or she thinks that there is sufficient reason for resuming it. It cannot be resumed until after 28 days have passed since either the date that the Lord Chancellor has notified to the senior coroner as the date of conclusion of the inquiry or, where the senior coroner has received no such notification, the date of publication of the findings of the inquiry.

118.   *Paragraphs 9(3), 9(5), 9(7) and 9(9)* are relevant where the senior coroner becomes aware during the course of the suspension of his investigation that criminal proceedings are under way of a type that would require a suspension under paragraph 2. Under *paragraphs 9(4), 9(6), 9(8) and 9(10)* the investigation may not be resumed before such criminal proceedings have ended unless a prosecuting authority or the Director of Service Prosecutions (as the case may be) has told the senior coroner that there is no objection to the investigation being resumed.

119.   *Paragraph 9(11)* prevents the resumed senior coroner's investigation from reaching a conclusion which is inconsistent with the outcome of the inquiry which triggered the suspension or any criminal proceedings that had to be concluded before it could be resumed. For example, if the outcome of an inquiry was a finding that a particular individual had committed suicide, a senior coroner's investigation cannot conclude that the particular individual was unlawfully killed.

Paragraph 10: Resumption of investigation under paragraph 5
120.   *Paragraph 10* of Schedule 1 states that where an investigation is suspended under paragraph 5, it may be resumed at any time the senior coroner thinks there is sufficient reason for resuming the investigation.

Paragraph 11: Supplemental

121.   *Paragraph 11(1)* of Schedule 1 requires that where a senior coroner resumes an investigation under Schedule 1, the senior coroner must resume any inquest that was adjourned under paragraph 6.

122.   Where an inquest is resumed, by *paragraph 11(3)* the resumed inquest may be held with a jury if the senior coroner thinks there is sufficient reason for doing so.

123.   Under *paragraph 11(4)*, if the inquest was started with a jury and then adjourned and the senior coroner decides to hold the resumed inquest with a jury, if at least seven members of the original jury are available to serve, then they will form the jury for the resumed inquest. If not, or the original jury was discharged, a new jury is required to be summoned.

Section 12: Investigation in Scotland

124.   This section makes provision for the Secretary of State or Chief Coroner to notify the Lord Advocate that he or she thinks that it may be appropriate for a service-related death which occurred abroad to be investigated under the Fatal Accidents and Sudden Deaths Inquiry (Scotland) Act 1976. It should be read with section 1A of that Act, which is inserted by section 50(2), discussed at paragraphs 320 to 323

125.   *Subsection (1)* provides that the section applies to deaths outside the UK of a person specified in *subsection (2) or (3)*.

126.   *Subsection (2)* specifies the service personnel that are covered, namely members of the regular and reserve forces who, when they die, are subject to service law (which governs all members of the armed forces) under section 367 of the Armed Forces Act 2006, and are on active service, preparing for or supporting active service, or engaged in training for active service.

127.   *Subsection (3)* adds that persons are covered if, when they die, they are not subject to service law but are, under paragraph 7 of Schedule 15 to the Armed Forces Act 2006 (persons designated by or on behalf of the Defence Council), civilians subject to service discipline; and are accompanying service personnel on active service.

128.   *Subsection (4)* provides that, if the body (of someone defined in subsections (2) and (3)) is already in Scotland, or is expected to be brought to the UK, and the Secretary of State thinks that it may be appropriate for the death to be investigated under the 1976 Act, he or she may notify the Lord Advocate in Scotland of this. In such circumstances the Secretary of State has no role, other than notifying the Lord Advocate.

129.   *Subsection (5)* provides that, if the body is England or Wales, and the Chief Coroner thinks that it may be appropriate for the death to be investigated under the 1976 Act, he or she may notify the Lord Advocate in Scotland of this.

130. "Active service" is defined in section 48(1) to mean service in an action or operation against an enemy; an operation outside the British Islands for the protection of life or property; or the military occupation of a foreign country or territory.

Section 13: Investigation in England and Wales despite body being brought to Scotland
131. There may be cases where the Lord Advocate initially decides that it would be appropriate for a Fatal Accident Inquiry to be held into the circumstances of the death but, for whatever reason, the Lord Advocate reverses this decision. In those circumstances the Lord Advocate can notify the Chief Coroner that it may be appropriate for an investigation to take place in England and Wales. An example may be that the family may have moved to England before the inquiry has taken place or other circumstances have changed which indicate that an investigation in England or Wales is more appropriate.

132. *Subsection (1)* enables the Chief Coroner to direct a senior coroner in England or Wales to conduct an investigation into a death where a body has been brought back to Scotland. The power to make such a direction exists if the deceased is a person who, when he or she died, was subject to service law under section 367 of the Armed Forces Act 2006 and was on active service, preparing for or supporting active service, or engaged in training for active service. It also covers where the deceased was a person not subject to service law but, by virtue of paragraph 7 of Schedule 15 to the 2006 Act, was a civilian subject to service discipline who was accompanying persons subject to service law who were engaged in active service. Secondly, the Lord Advocate must have been notified by the Secretary of State or the Chief Coroner that it may be appropriate for the death to be investigated under the 1976 Act. Thirdly, the body must have been brought to Scotland.

133. Fourthly, no Fatal Accident Inquiry must have taken place (or, if one has been started, it must not yet have finished). Fifthly the Lord Advocate must have advised the Chief Coroner that in the Lord Advocate's view, it may be appropriate for a coroner investigation, in England or Wales, to take place. Lastly, the Chief Coroner must have reason to suspect that the duty to investigate deaths under section 1 (which applies to deaths in England and Wales) would apply to the death, namely that the deceased died a violent or unnatural death; the cause of death being unknown; or the deceased died in custody or other state detention. If all those circumstances apply to a death the Chief Coroner may direct a coroner in England or Wales to conduct an investigation. Any coroner given such a direction must conduct an investigation into the death, subject to section 3.

Section 14: Post-mortem examinations
134. This section sets out the arrangements for ordering post-mortem examinations, and makes slightly different provision from that contained in sections 19 and 20 of the 1988 Act.

135. *Subsection (1)* gives a senior coroner power to ask a suitable practitioner to make a post-mortem examination of a body if the senior coroner is either responsible for conducting an investigation into the death or a post-mortem examination will enable the senior coroner to decide if he or she has a duty under section 1 to conduct an investigation. This may be relevant where it is not clear whether a death occurred as a result of a notifiable disease or whether a child was stillborn – where, for example, an infant's body is found and it is not

clear whether it ever had independent life. Where it is known or established that a child was stillborn, the senior coroner will have no further power to carry out an investigation.

136.   The term "post-mortem examination" is not defined but it will include any examination made of the deceased including non-invasive examinations, for example, using Magnetic Resonance Imaging (MRI) scans.

137.   The 1988 Act makes a distinction between post-mortem and "special" examinations (the latter are a more specific kind of post-mortem examination and would include toxicology tests to establish whether, for example, alcohol or drugs were in the bloodstream). The Act removes this distinction, enabling the senior coroner to detail the kind of examination he or she would like the practitioner to make – for example, to ask for a particular examination of a tissue or organ which seems most relevant to the cause of death if a full post-mortem is not considered necessary *(subsection (2))*.

138.   *Subsection (3)* defines a suitable practitioner as either a registered medical practitioner or, where a particular form of examination is required, a practitioner who is of a type or description the Chief Coroner has designated as suitably qualified and competent to carry out such examinations.

139.   *Subsection (4)* ensures that any medical practitioner about whom there are allegations in relation to the death is not able to carry out the examination of the body, although such a person may be represented at an examination.

140.   *Subsection (5)* requires the person making the examination to report the result to the senior coroner as soon as is practicable.

Section 15: Power to remove body
141.   This section specifies the arrangements for moving a body to a different location, for example to enable a post-mortem examination to be carried out.

142.   Under *subsection (1)* a senior coroner who is responsible for conducting an investigation into the death or who needs to request a post-mortem examination in order to decide if he or she has a duty under section 1 to conduct an investigation may order that the body be moved to any suitable place. (The notes to section 14 set out when a senior coroner may need to request a post-mortem examination in order to decide if he or she has a duty under section 1 to conduct an investigation.)

143.   This removes the restriction in section 22(1) of the 1988 Act that a body can be moved only within a senior coroner's area or to an immediately adjoining area which has caused practical difficulties in a major incident where there have been several deaths. This power will also allow a senior coroner to make use of specialist equipment or skills available in a different part of the country and may, on occasion, mean that full post-mortems can be avoided.

144.   The body can be moved to a place which is outside the senior coroner's area only with the consent of the person providing that place (for example, a mortuary manager) except in the case of local authority premises. The issue of costs will be dealt with in regulations made under section 43.

Section 16: Investigations lasting more than a year
145.   *Subsection (1)* places a duty on a senior coroner to notify the Chief Coroner of any investigation that has not been completed within a year of the date on which the coroner was made aware of the death. The coroner must then tell the Chief Coroner when an investigation which has taken more than a year is finally completed or discontinued. *Subsection (3)* gives the Chief Coroner a duty to keep a register of the investigations that take over 12 months to complete. See too section 36(4)(a) as regards reports to the Lord Chancellor relating to investigations lasting more than a year.

Section 17:   Monitoring of and training for investigations into deaths of service personnel
146.   This section gives the Chief Coroner the duty to monitor investigations into the deaths of service personnel and to ensure that coroners are suitably trained to conduct such investigations.

Chapter 2: Notification, certification and registration of deaths

Section 18: Notification by medical practitioner to senior coroner
147.   This section enables regulations to be made by the Lord Chancellor requiring a registered medical practitioner to notify a senior coroner of certain categories of death of which they become aware.

Section 19: Medical examiners
148.   This section relates to the appointment of, and functions to be carried out by, medical examiners. It also enables regulations to be made by the Secretary of State for Health (in relation to England) and the relevant Welsh Ministers (in relation to Wales) about the appointment, payment and training of, and functions to be carried out by, medical examiners.

149.   *Subsection (1)* requires Primary Care Trusts (PCTs) in England and Local Health Boards (LHBs) in Wales to appoint medical examiners to discharge the functions given to them by this Chapter.

150.   *Subsection (2)(a)* specifies that PCTs and LHBs must appoint enough medical examiners and make available enough funds and other resources (including medical examiners' officers) to enable the medical examiners to discharge their functions in the area served by the PCT or LHB.

151.   Under *subsection (2)(b)*, medical examiners will be monitored by their PCT or LHB as to whether or not they meet expected standards or levels of performance in carrying out their work as medical examiners. This monitoring needs to be considered alongside the requirement in *subsection (5)* for PCTs and LHBs to take no role in relation to the way that medical examiners exercise their professional judgment as medical practitioners.

152.   *Subsection (3)* specifies, subject to regulations under subsection (4)(f), that medical examiners must, at the time of appointment, be fully registered medical practitioners for the previous five years and be practising at the time of appointment or have practiced within the previous five years.

153.   Regulations made under *subsection (4)(a)* will specify terms of appointment for medical examiners and allow for the termination of their appointment. Whilst medical examiners will, for the most part, confirm or establish the cause of death for deaths that have occurred in the area served by the PCT or LHB by whom they have been appointed, they may be asked to scrutinise deaths in other areas.

154.   Regulations made under *subsection (4)(b)* will specify what payments may be made to medical examiners by way of remuneration, expenses, fees, compensation for termination of appointment, pensions, allowances or gratuities. Such payments would be in line with arrangements applying in the specific area in respect of remuneration and those applying nationally in respect of other similar payments.

155.   Regulations made under *subsection (4)(c)* will specify the training that medical examiners must have successfully completed prior to their appointment and the training that they need to undertake during the term of their appointment.

156.   Regulations made under *subsection (4)(d)* will make provision about the procedure to be followed by medical examiners in carrying out their functions with a view to ensuring that they are able to carry out independent scrutiny of medical certificates of cause of death (MCCDs) and do so in a way that is robust, proportionate, and consistent. The regulations may also provide that, in order to help ensure their professional independence, medical examiners will not be allowed to confirm or establish the cause of death of any person to whom they are related or with whom they have had any fiduciary relationship; and that they will not be allowed to scrutinise MCCDs prepared by any doctor with whom they have a close working or professional relationship or with whom they have an established fiduciary relationship (see also section 20).

157.   Regulations made under *subsection (4)(e)* may provide for the functions of medical examiners to be extended or changed to support future developments of the service.

158.   Regulations made under *subsection (4)(f)* may provide for the functions of medical examiners to be carried out by persons not meeting the criteria in subsection (3) during a period of emergency certified by the Secretary of State in accordance with subsection (7). (See also section 20(4) for a related provision allowing the MCCD to be given during a period of emergency by a registered medical practitioner who has not attended the deceased before his or her death and is therefore not the "attending practitioner".)

159.   *Subsection (5)* specifies that PCTs and LHBs must allow medical examiners to exercise their own professional judgement as medical practitioners in deciding, for example, whether to confirm individual causes of death or refer them to a senior coroner. This provision needs to be read together with the obligation on PCTs and LHBs to monitor medical examiners in *subsection (2)* and the procedures to be prescribed by regulations under subsection (4)(d).

160.   *Subsections (8)* and *(9)* make provision concerning periods of emergency certified by the Secretary of State under *subsection (7)*.

Section 20: Medical certificate of cause of death
161.   This section enables the Secretary of State for Health to make regulations about the preparation, scrutiny and confirmation of MCCDs and about the way the confirmed MCCD is notified and given to a registrar or about how the death is referred to a senior coroner. The section also enables regulations to be made about the payment of a fee for the service provided by a medical examiner.

162.   The independent scrutiny and confirmation of MCCDs is part of a wider process that starts with the preparation of the certificate by a registered medical practitioner who attended the deceased and ends with the certificate being returned to the medical examiner after it has been used by the registrar to register the death. The new unified process is intended to be simpler and more transparent than the previous one and requires specification of activities, responsibilities and alternative scenarios that are more suited to regulations than to provisions on the face of the Act. *Subsection (1)* provides the power to make the necessary regulations.

163.   The new process has been designed with the active engagement of a wide range of stakeholders and is illustrated in an overview booklet published by the Department of Health (http://www.dh.gov.uk/en/Publicationsandstatistics/ Publications/PublicationsPolicyAndGuidance/DH_090533).

164.   Regulations made under *subsection (1)(a)* will require a registered medical practitioner who attended the deceased prior to death (the "attending practitioner") to prepare an MCCD (the "attending practitioner's certificate") stating the cause of death to the best of the practitioner's knowledge and belief. This duty has been transferred and adapted from section 22 of the Births and Deaths Registration Act 1953 (the 1953 Act) (see *subsections (1)(m)* and *(3)* for the associated transfer of responsibility for prescribing forms, including the MCCD, and for making them available to medical practitioners).

165.   The attending practitioner's certificate will be prepared using first-hand knowledge of the deceased's condition prior to death together with information from medical notes and patient records. PCTs (in England), LHBs (in Wales) and healthcare providers (both in the NHS and the private sector) will also be encouraged to adopt local protocols relating to the verification of the fact of death that are able to provide the attending practitioner with information on circumstances leading to the death. Knowledge of these circumstances may assist the attending practitioner in establishing the cause of death or in deciding that the death needs to be referred to a senior coroner.

166.   Where the attending practitioner needs advice on how to complete an MCCD or wants to discuss the probable cause of death before preparing the certificate, he or she will be able to speak with a medical examiner. This is expected to reduce the number of deaths that are unnecessarily reported to a senior coroner.

167.   If the attending practitioner is unable to establish the cause of death, or is unable to do so in a period of time prescribed by regulations made under *subsection (2)(a)*, then the death must be referred to a senior coroner.

168.   If the attending practitioner is not contactable within a period of time after death prescribed by regulations that may be made under subsection (2)(a), then the death must be referred to a senior coroner. This is relevant, in particular, to deaths in the community, which, even though they are apparently due to natural causes, occur at a time when the deceased's usual doctor is not contactable.

169.   If there is no attending practitioner, for example, where the deceased person was not receiving treatment for the condition that caused the death then the provisions under subsection (1)(a) do not apply and the death must be notified to a senior coroner as prescribed by regulations that may be made under section 18.

170.   It is intended that regulations made under subsection (1)(a) will specify that an attending practitioner's certificate will not be required where the death has been notified to a senior coroner in accordance with regulations made under section 18 and is investigated by the senior coroner as specified in section 1. This is a key change from the previous process and addresses a long-standing issue in which a strict interpretation of the 1953 Act requires an attending practitioner to prepare a certificate even if he or she cannot establish the cause of death, and requires the registrar to refer this certificate to a coroner.

171.   Section 18 together with regulations under *subsection (1)(a)(ii)* change the practice of medical practitioners to refer deaths to a senior coroner into a statutory duty.

172.   It is intended that regulations made under *subsection (1)(b)* will require that where an attending practitioner's certificate has been prepared, the hospital bereavement office or GP surgery (or equivalent) must transmit a copy of it to a medical examiner's office. The original certificate will be held by the hospital bereavement office or GP surgery (or equivalent) until it has been scrutinised and confirmed by a medical examiner. This is a key change to the previous process in which, if there is no local protocol to the contrary, the

attending practitioner's certificate is given to the family immediately after it is written. The Government expects that the additional time required to complete the scrutiny will in most cases be no longer than the time taken to complete the forms previously required by the Cremation (England and Wales) Regulations 2008. There is no requirement to complete these forms in the new process.

173.   Regulations made under *subsection (1)(c)* will allow registrars to invite a medical examiner to request a fresh attending practitioner's certificate. A fresh certificate may be required if, during registration, the informant provides new information about the death which invalidates the cause of death previously confirmed by the medical examiner. The provisions outlined here allow registrars to retain their duty to provide a last check that a death does not need to be notified to a senior coroner. However, many registrars find it difficult to perform this role – particularly where they have to refer a substantial number of certificates – because they have to rely on knowledge gained through experience and because the delays caused to bereaved families can cause considerable stress. The new process is designed to address this issue and to reduce significantly the number of MCCDs that registrars need to refer to senior coroners.

174.   Regulations made under *subsection (1)(d)* will allow arrangements to be established in relation to deaths that senior coroners refer to medical examiners. These will be the deaths that were originally notified to a senior coroner under section 18 or referred to a senior coroner under subsection (1)(a)(ii) that the senior coroner has decided not to investigate. In these cases, the senior coroner will issue a form stating that he or she has no further interest in the death and will transmit this form to the medical examiner's office together with any relevant information about the death that he or she has used in coming to his or her decision. In some cases, this information may include advice provided by a medical examiner in response to a request from the senior coroner or coroner's officer.

175.   Since the senior coroner can refer a death to a medical examiner only where the cause of death is known, the regulations made under subsection (1)(a)(i) will allow the attending practitioner to prepare an attending practitioner's certificate. If there is no attending practitioner or if the attending practitioner is not available within a prescribed period after a senior coroner decides not to investigate, then a medical examiner will establish the cause of death and prepare a "medical examiner's certificate" as specified in regulations made under *subsection (1)(h)(i).* These changes remove the current situation in which some deaths need to be registered as "uncertified".

176.   Regulations may be made under *subsection (1)(e)* requiring a medical examiner to make whatever enquiries appear to be necessary in order to confirm or establish the cause of death. Whilst medical examiners will have full access to medical notes and patient records as a result of the amendment to the Access to Health Records Act 1990 made by paragraph 29 of Schedule 21, they will not be able to require any individual or organisation to respond to their enquiries or provide information. If a medical examiner is not able to obtain information required to confirm or establish the cause of death, then the death will be referred to a senior coroner (as outlined below) and the senior coroner will be able to require the information to be provided.

177.   When the copy of an attending practitioner's certificate is received by a medical examiner's office from a hospital bereavement office or GP's surgery (or equivalent) it should be accompanied by relevant medical notes and/or patient records. Where these cannot be transmitted or provided easily, arrangements may be made for a medical examiner to view them in situ. A medical examiner's officer will ensure that the attending practitioner's certificate has been completed and that the associated notes and records have been provided or are available and then, if necessary, contact the deceased person's next of kin, or other appropriate person or people, to obtain any further information required. The medical examiner's officer will talk with the bereaved family, usually by telephone, in a way that does not intrude on their grief or raise concerns that would otherwise not exist. As a further safeguard against unnecessary intrusion, information collected by bereavement officers or, for reported deaths that a senior coroner has decided not to investigate, by coroners' officers, will be made available to the medical examiner's officer.

178.   If the attending practitioner's certificate has been completed properly, it will advise that the attending practitioner or another prescribed person has seen, identified and externally examined the deceased person's body after death. The purpose of this examination is to confirm there are no injuries or other suspicious features that might indicate an unnatural death. If, in exceptional circumstances agreed with a medical examiner, the attending practitioner has not been able to see, identify and examine the body, then the medical examiner will need to arrange to do so during scrutiny. A medical examiner will also need to see, identify and examine the body for deaths that are referred to him or her by a senior coroner and which require a medical examiner's certificate as set out in subsection (1)(d).

179.   Regulations may be made under *subsection (1)(f)* requiring a medical examiner, after scrutinising the attending practitioner's certificate and other information prepared by the medical examiner's officer, either to confirm the cause of death or to refer the death to the senior coroner.

180.   In order to ensure that the scrutiny carried out by the medical examiner is robust, proportionate and consistent, there will be a protocol that recognises different levels of risk depending on the setting, stated cause and circumstances. The protocol will establish the minimum level of scrutiny for specific situations but will allow a medical examiner to use professional judgement to determine the degree to which the scrutiny is pursued.

181.   If, during scrutiny, a medical examiner is unable to confirm the cause of death or decides that it meets any of the criteria prescribed in regulations made under section 18, then the death will be referred to a senior coroner as specified in regulations made under *subsection (1)(h)(ii)* or section 18. The medical examiner will give reasons for the referral and, where appropriate, suggest what type of post-mortem may be necessary.   If, in exceptional cases, the senior coroner decides not to investigate the death and cannot come to an agreement with the medical examiner about the cause of death then the case would need to be taken through the appeals process as set out in Chapter 6 of Part 1 of the Act. The medical examiner has been included as an "interested person" in section 47 in relation to this appeals process.

182.   If, during scrutiny, a medical examiner forms the opinion that the cause of death stated on the attending practitioner's certificate is either insufficient or incorrect, but the death is not reportable to a senior coroner, the medical examiner will discuss the death with the attending practitioner and invite him or her to prepare a fresh certificate.   The Government intends that this will be specified in regulations made under subsection (1)(c). If, in exceptional cases, the attending practitioner and medical examiner are unable to agree on the cause of death, the medical examiner will refer the case to a senior coroner.

183.   Once any issues raised by the next of kin (or other appropriate person or people) have been resolved, they will be advised that the MCCD can be collected from the hospital bereavement office or GP Surgery (or equivalent) or, for an MCCD prepared by a medical examiner, from the medical examiner's office.   At the same time, a medical examiner's authorisation will be transmitted to the attending practitioner (if one exists) and the registrar to notify them that the cause of death has been confirmed and that the MCCD can be issued and used to register the death.

184.   A copy of the medical examiner's authorisation will be transmitted to funeral directors to allow them to finish preparing the body for burial or cremation where this involves changing the body in a way that might render it unsuitable for a post-mortem.

185.   Regulations may be made under *subsection (1)(g)* about giving the MCCD to a registrar. In practice, the MCCD will be given to an informant or someone collecting it on behalf of the informant and the informant will give the MCCD to a registrar. The regulations may allow the MCCD to be given in other ways: for example, sent by secure post to the informant or sent directly to a registrar. These arrangements are intended to ensure that the new process is as fast and as convenient as possible.

186.   The policy intention is that registrars must wait until they have received (or can access) a copy of the medical examiner's authorisation before they can accept (or confirm acceptance of): a request to register a death; a request to defer registration; or a request to authorise disposal before registration.

187.   Where a medical examiner has issued a certificate by virtue of regulations under *subsection (1)(h)* after referral of the case to him or her by a senior coroner (see subsection (1)(d)), further provisions, made by regulations under *subsections (1)(i) and (j)*, will apply. These provisions will correspond to those made under subsection (1)(c) and (g) in relation to an attending practitioner's certificate that has been confirmed by the medical examiner in accordance with regulations under subsection (1)(f).

188.   Once scrutiny has been completed, a medical examiner or someone acting on behalf of a medical examiner (usually the medical examiner's officer) will speak with the next of kin of the deceased person (or other appropriate person or people) to advise them of the outcome of the scrutiny. This conversation will be required by regulations made under *subsection (1)(k)*.

189.   Where the cause of death has been confirmed, the medical examiner or person acting on his or her behalf will explain the cause of death and check that it does not raise any issues that have not yet been considered. If issues are raised and cannot be resolved during the conversation then the medical examiner may decide to re-open the scrutiny or refer the death to the senior coroner.

190.   Regulations may be made under *subsection (1)(l)* requiring the person nominated as the informant for the purpose of registration, or another prescribed person, to confirm in writing that a medical examiner or someone acting on his or her behalf (usually the medical examiner's officer) has explained the confirmed cause of death as set out in subsection (1)(k). At present, the Government anticipates that this written confirmation will be provided during registration; however, there are other possible options.   The purpose of the written confirmation is to provide evidence that the cause of death has been explained to the informant or other prescribed person, thereby lending transparency to the new process in contrast to that provided by the previous process.

191.   Regulations made under *subsection (1)(m)* will enable the Secretary of State for Health, after consultation as set out in subsection (3), to prescribe forms, including the "MCCD" form. The regulations will also require the forms to be made available to medical examiners, registered medical practitioners and others who need to use them.

192.   Regulations made under *subsection (1)(n)* will require the Chief Medical Officer of the Department of Health to issue guidance as to how certificates and other forms are to be completed and to do so after consulting the person who holds the office with corresponding functions in relation to Wales, as well as the Registrar General and the Statistics Board.

193.   Regulations made under *subsection (1)(o)* will enable all forms, including the MCCD form, to be signed or otherwise authenticated. Authentication in this context will enable the forms to be transmitted or made available electronically.

194.   *Subsection (2)(a)* enables any regulation in *subsection (1)* that imposes a requirement to have a prescribed period within which the requirement is to be complied with.

195.   *Subsection (2)(b)* enables any regulation in *subsection (1)* that imposes a requirement to have prescribed cases or circumstances in which the requirement does, or does not, apply. This provision may need to be used, in particular, during periods of emergency as defined in section 17(7).

196.   *Subsection (3)* requires the Secretary of State for Health to consult with Welsh Ministers, the Registrar General and the Statistics Board before prescribing forms, including the MCCD form, as specified in *subsection (1)(m)*.   The Statistics Board will continue to ensure that the MCCD form complies with requirements set by the World Health Organisation.

197.   *Subsection (4)* allows regulations under *subsection (1)* to provide that functions otherwise exercisable by attending practitioners to be carried out during a period of emergency by registered medical practitioners who did not attend the deceased prior to death. The primary activities to which this would relate are the preparation of an MCCD and discussion with a medical examiner about any changes that might be required in order for the cause of death to be confirmed (see also section 19(4)(f) on when functions normally carried out by medical examiners may be carried out by others during a period of emergency).

198.   *Subsection (5)* enables regulations to be made by the Secretary of State for Health (for England) and Welsh Ministers (for Wales) to provide for a fee to be payable to a PCT or LHB in respect of a medical examiner's scrutiny and confirmation of an attending practitioner's certificate or the preparation and issue of a medical examiner's certificate. The fee level will be set on the basis of full cost recovery, without any element of profit. The first such regulations, and any subsequent regulations that raise fees by more than the rate of inflation, will be subject to the affirmative resolution procedure: see subsection (4)(a) and (5)(a) of section 176.

199.   Funeral arrangers currently pay a total of £160.50 to individual doctors for the preparation and issue of forms required under the Cremation (England and Wales) Regulations 2008. In the new system, the medical examiner will perform the function of all three of these doctors and will, the Government expects, be able to do so at a lower total cost. An analysis of costs and benefits is available in the Department of Health's Impact Assessment   (http://www.dh.gov.uk/en/Consultations   /Closed consultations/DH_076971).

200.   Under *subsection (6)*, the Secretary of State will not need to make regulations about cremation (under the Cremation Act 1902) if they are unnecessary because of other regulations made under Part 1 of this Act, or provision contained in or made under Part 2 of the the 1953 Act in relation to England and Wales.

Section 21: National Medical Examiner
201.   Section 21 allows the Secretary of State to appoint a National Medical Examiner (NME). The NME will issue guidance to medical examiners with a view to securing that they carry out their functions in an effective and proportionate manner. Further functions can be conferred on the NME by regulations. Medical examiners will be required to have regard to that guidance when carrying out their functions.

202.   The NME will be appointed by the Secretary of State for Health following consultation with Welsh Ministers who would also be consulted when further functions are conferred on the NME and before the NME issues guidance to medical examiners. The appointment of the NME will be on such terms and conditions as the Secretary of State for Health considers appropriate.

Chapter 3: Coroner areas, appointments etc

Section 22 and Schedule 2: Coroner areas
203.   This section gives effect to Schedule 2 which provides for England and Wales to be divided into coroner areas and gives the Lord Chancellor the power to set and alter the boundaries of these areas (by order subject to the negative resolution procedure) after consultation with the relevant local authorities, Welsh Ministers, and any other persons the Lord Chancellor thinks appropriate. Each coroner area will cover either the whole of one local authority area or the whole of two or more local authority areas (although this provision will not apply in relation to coroner areas specified in the transitional order made under paragraph 1(1) of Schedule 22).

204.   Where the area includes two or more local authorities (*paragraph 3 of Schedule 2*), one of them will be the lead authority for the area, known as the "relevant authority". If the local authorities cannot agree which of them should be the relevant authority, the Lord Chancellor will decide on their behalf, consulting the Secretary of State for Communities and Local Government in respect of local authorities in England, and Welsh Ministers in respect of local authorities in Wales.

205.   The Lord Chancellor may alter, by order subject to the negative resolution procedure, and change the names of, coroner areas using a similar consultation procedure.

206.   The Schedule also makes provision in *paragraph 4* in relation to bodies which are situated outside the senior coroner's area. Once a senior coroner is responsible for conducting an investigation into a death, the fact that the body is outside that coroner's area does not change his or her functions in relation to the death or give another senior coroner any functions in relation to the death. This is broadly equivalent to the provision in section 22(3) of the 1988 Act.

Section 23 and Schedule 3: Appointment etc of senior coroners, area coroners and assistant coroners
207.   This section gives effect to Schedule 3 which sets out the procedure for the appointment of coroners, qualifications required and terms of office. It also makes provision for the exercise of a senior coroner's functions by area and assistant coroners.

Part 1 – Appointment of senior, area and assistant coroners
208.   The Act will change the titles of the office of coroner. The hierarchy under the 1988 Act consisted (in descending order) of coroners, deputy coroners and assistant deputy coroners. Under the Act, there will be senior coroners, area coroners and assistant coroners.

209.   Under the 1988 Act, the relevant local authority appointed coroners (but not deputy and assistant coroners). The Secretary of State approved certain coroners' appointments; and where the coroner's district consisted of two or more such areas, or two or more Welsh principal areas, the relevant local authority consulted the others before making an appointment. The coroner appointed his or her own deputy and any assistant deputy coroners (section 6 of the 1988 Act). This will not continue under the Act.

210.   Under Part 1 of Schedule 3 appointments of all coroners are made by the relevant authority for each coroner area. There is a new requirement for the Lord Chancellor and Chief Coroner to consent to the appointment of all senior coroners.

211.   Following consultation with the Chief Coroner and the relevant local authorities, the Lord Chancellor can determine whether the coroner area requires one or more area coroners in addition to the senior coroner, and if so how many. He or she can also determine the minimum number of assistant coroners.

Part 2 – Qualifications of senior, area and assistant coroners
212.   Under this Act, all coroners must be legally qualified. Previously, under the 1988 Act (section 2(1)(b)), being a legally qualified medical practitioner of five years' standing also sufficed. Transitional arrangements are to be made so that paragraph 3 of Part 2 does not apply in relation to those coroners treated as appointed under the transitional arrangements made in the Act.

213.   This Part also disqualifies local councillors from appointment as coroners, if the area in respect of which they were elected falls within the coroner area.

Part 3 – Vacancies, and functions of area and assistant coroners
214.   Part 3 of Schedule 3 makes provision for filling vacancies on the resignation, dismissal or retirement of coroners, and the arrangements for filling posts on a temporary basis. This Part also provides that area coroners and assistant coroners can perform any functions of the senior coroner when he or she is absent or unavailable or otherwise with the senior coroner's consent.

Part 4 - Terms of office of senior, area and assistant coroners
215.   Part 4 of Schedule 3 introduces a new retirement age of 70 for coroners and sets out the procedure for resignation from office. A coroner is no longer to be regarded as holding a "freehold office".

216.   It also gives the Lord Chancellor the power to remove a senior coroner, area coroner or assistant coroner from office if that coroner is incapable of performing his or her functions or is guilty of misbehaviour. Before he or she can exercise this power, the Lord Chancellor must have the agreement of the Lord Chief Justice.

217.   Part 4 also provides for senior coroners, area coroners and assistant coroners to be subject to the disciplinary provisions of Chapter 3 of Part 4 of the Constitutional Reform Act 2005 (which includes the power for the Lord Chief Justice to issue reprimands).

218.   It makes provision for the relevant authority for the area to pay salaries to senior coroners and area coroners and fees to assistant coroners. The amount of these salaries and fees is for the relevant coroner and the relevant authority to agree. If they fail to reach an agreement the matter can be referred to the Lord Chancellor, who can determine the amount.

219.   This Part also requires the relevant authority for an area to make provision for pensions for senior and area coroners.

220.   Additional terms of office can be agreed between the appropriate authority and the coroner.

Section 24: Provision of staff and accommodation
221.   This section requires the relevant authority for a coroner area to provide sufficient administrative staff and coroners' officers. When, locally, the police authority is responsible for providing coroners' officers, then they will be expected to continue to do so. The local authority and local police authority will be expected to work together, with the senior coroner, to secure appropriate staffing levels. (Police authorities currently provide 90% of coroner's officers to support the work of coroners.)

222.   The relevant authority is also obliged to provide, or secure the provision of, accommodation to enable senior coroners to carry out their functions. This accommodation must either be maintained by the relevant authority or they must secure that it is maintained. This does not apply if another person has responsibility for maintaining the accommodation. This recognises that not all coroners have a dedicated court to hold inquests and that there will continue to be a need to hire such facilities in the future, including court accommodation where the existing court room is insufficient for the purposes of a particular inquest. Under section 31 of the 1988 Act, the relevant council had power to provide accommodation for inquests.

223.   The relevant authority is required to take into account the views of the senior coroner when providing and, where relevant, maintaining accommodation. The Act allows inquests to be held anywhere in England and Wales so that there is new flexibility if particular inquests have requirements for the sort of accommodation which is not available within the coroner's own area. The expectation will be, however, that an inquest is normally held within the area of the coroner who is conducting the investigation.

Chapter 4: Investigations concerning Treasure

Section 25 and Schedule 4: Coroner for Treasure and Assistant Coroners for Treasure
224.   This section gives effect to Schedule 4 which sets out the procedure for the appointment of the new Coroner for Treasure, qualifications required and terms of office. It also makes provision for the exercise of the Coroner for Treasure's functions by assistant coroners who are designated as Assistant Coroners for Treasure.

Part 1 – Appointment, qualifications and terms of office of Coroner for Treasure
225.   *Paragraph 1* allows the Lord Chancellor to appoint a person as the Coroner for Treasure. This is a new role; the Coroner for Treasure will investigate all finds believed to be treasure or treasure trove from across England and Wales. Although he or she will have an office in a particular location, the location for any inquest required as part of a treasure investigation will take into account the convenience of interested persons, including the finder and the landowner.

226.   The qualification to become the Coroner for Treasure will be the same legal qualification that is used for senior coroners (*paragraph 2*). Senior coroners will therefore be able to apply to become the Coroner for Treasure.

227.   *Paragraphs 3 to 6* set out how the Coroner for Treasure may vacate the office and how the Lord Chancellor may, with the Lord Chief Justice's agreement, remove the Coroner for Treasure for incapacity or misbehaviour. They also provide for the Lord Chancellor to remunerate the Coroner for Treasure as appropriate.

Part 2 – Designation and remuneration of Assistant Coroners for Treasure

228.   One or more assistant coroners will be designated as Assistant Coroners for Treasure (*paragraph 7*). They will cease to be Assistant Coroners for Treasure if they cease to be assistant coroners (*paragraph 9*).

Part 3 – Miscellaneous

229.   Under *paragraph 11*, an Assistant Coroner for Treasure may undertake any of the functions of the Coroner for Treasure, should he or she be absent or unavailable or with the consent of the Coroner for Treasure. The Lord Chancellor will also be able to appoint staff to carry out the administrative functions related to treasure investigations (*paragraph 12*).

Section 26: Investigations concerning treasure

230.   The Coroner for Treasure will investigate items which are reported to his or her office under section 8 of the Treasure Act 1996 (1996 Act), and may do so if there is suspicion about an object which has not been reported. This will be to establish whether or not the object is treasure or treasure trove, and if so, who found it, where and when it was found.

231.   *Subsection (6)* sets out that senior coroners, area coroners and assistant coroners have no functions in relation to these objects, unless the assistant coroner has been designated as an Assistant Coroner for Treasure. This means that there will be a single reporting point for all treasure finds across England and Wales, and a single point of investigation.

Section 27: Inquests concerning treasure

232.   As part of an investigation, the Coroner for Treasure may hold an inquest into an object; many treasure investigations do not however require an inquest. *Subsection (2)* requires the Coroner for Treasure to hold the inquest without a jury unless there is sufficient reason for one. The number of jurors and the way in which the jury will arrive at its determination mirrors the provisions for death investigations in sections 8 and 9.

Section 28: Outcome of investigations concerning treasure

233.   This section sets out how the Coroner for Treasure must make treasure determinations, depending on the type of investigation.

Section 29: Exception to duty to investigate

234.   This section extends the circumstances in which the Crown or relevant franchisee may disclaim title to an object to allow notice to be given to the Coroner for Treasure disclaiming the title before it is determined that the object is treasure. The finder in these circumstances would not be compensated under the treasure valuation system, but the object would be returned to the finder for them to dispose of as they see fit. Franchisees – where the item will vest in the franchisee rather than the Crown – are the Duchy of Cornwall, the Duchy of Lancaster, the Corporation of the City of London and the City of Bristol.

Section 30: Duty to notify Coroner for Treasure etc of acquisition of certain objects

235.   This section inserts a new section 8A into the 1996 Act, imposing a duty on acquirers of objects which might be treasure to report them to the Coroner for Treasure. The object will be investigated and the usual determinations made about when, where and by whom it was found, and whether it is treasure. The acquirer – who might have bought the object, been given it or had it bequeathed to them – will be able to receive a reward from the Treasure Valuation Committee. Breach of the duty could lead to prosecution, with the penalties, on the commencement of section 280(2) of the 2003 Act, of 51 weeks imprisonment, a level 5 fine, or both.

Section 31: Code of practice under the Treasure Act 1996

236.   *Subsection (1)* allows the 1996 Act Code of Practice to be amended to make provision for circumstances where an object is disclaimed under section 29.

237.   *Subsection (2)* ensures that the Coroner for Treasure (or an Assistant Coroner for Treasure acting on his or her behalf) will not be liable in the civil courts if he or she acts in accordance with the Code of Practice.

Chapter 5: Further provisions to do with investigations and deaths

Section 32 and Schedule 5: Powers of coroners

238.   This section brings Schedule 5 into effect, which sets out the powers of senior coroners and the Coroner for Treasure (who has identical powers save for paragraph 7 which does not apply to the Coroner for Treasure).

Paragraph 1 and 2: Power to require evidence to be given or produced

239.   *Paragraph 1* of Schedule 5 gives a senior coroner power to summon witnesses and to compel the production of evidence for the purposes of an investigation.

240.   Under *paragraph 1(1)* a senior coroner may issue a notice requiring a person to attend at a given time and place to give evidence at an inquest or to produce any documents they have that are relevant to the inquest or to produce anything else they have that is relevant to the inquest so that it can be inspected, examined or tested.

241.   *Paragraph 1(2)* provides that the senior coroner can also notify someone that they must provide the senior coroner with a written statement, or produce any documents or anything else they have that the senior coroner considers is relevant to the investigation.

242.   *Paragraph 1(3)* sets out information which must be included in any notice that the senior coroner issues under paragraphs 1(1) or 1(2).

243.   *Paragraph 1(4)* gives those to whom the senior coroner has issued a notice under paragraph 1(1) or (2) the right to claim that he or she is unable to comply with the notice or that it is not reasonable for the senior coroner to ask him or her to do so. The senior coroner can cancel or amend the notice on that ground.

244.   Under *paragraph 1(5)*, when deciding whether to cancel or amend the notice, the senior coroner has to take into account the public interest of that information being available to the investigation or inquest.

245.   Under *paragraph 1(6)*, a document or thing is defined as being under a person's control if it is in that person's possession or if they have a right to possession of it.

246.   By *paragraph 1(7)*, the notice is not limited by the coroner's area and can therefore be issued to a person anywhere in England or Wales.

247.   *Paragraph 1(8)* extends the powers under paragraph 1 to the Coroner for Treasure when carrying out treasure investigations. This allows the Coroner for Treasure to order a person to produce an object believed to be treasure for examination and testing, for example.

248.   *Paragraph 2* of Schedule 5 makes it clear that the senior coroner does not have the power to require anything to be provided to him or her that a person could not be required to provide to a civil court, mirroring the restriction on many information gathering powers contained in existing legislation. The senior coroner also does not have the power to require evidence to be provided if this would be incompatible with European Union law. It is also made clear that the rules of law in relation to public interest immunity apply equally in relation to investigations or inquests under Part 1 of the Act.

Paragraphs 3 to 5: Power of entry, search and seizure
249.   *Paragraph 3* of Schedule 5 gives senior coroners a new, statutory power to enter and search land and seize items which are relevant to their investigations.

250.   By *paragraph 3(1)*, a senior coroner has a power to enter and search particular land if he or she has authorisation from the Chief Coroner or from a senior coroner nominated by the Chief Coroner to give such permission. A record must be made of all authorisations sought and given (*paragraph 4*). (The matters recorded under paragraph 4 have to be included in the Chief Coroner's annual report to the Lord Chancellor: see section 36(4)(c).)

251.   By *paragraph 3(2)*, the Chief Coroner, or a senior coroner to whom the power is delegated, may allow a coroner to enter and search premises only if that coroner has reason to suspect that there might be something on the premises relevant to the investigation. One of the conditions in *paragraph 3(3)* must also be met ie that the coroner must be unable to contact the person who could give permission to enter and search the premises; permission has already been refused; there is reason to believe that permission would be refused; or the purpose of the search would be frustrated or significantly prejudiced without immediate entry.

252.   Under *paragraph 3(4)* a senior coroner has a power to seize anything on the land, or inspect or take copies of any documents that are relevant to the investigation.

253.   *Paragraph 3(6)* extends the new statutory powers of entry, search and seizure to the Coroner for Treasure when investigating objects which may be treasure or treasure trove.

254.   Under *paragraph 5(1)*, the power to seize items, inspect and take copies of documents under paragraph 3(4) can only be used if the person exercising it has reasonable grounds to believe that its exercise might assist the investigation and, in relation to seizure, that it is necessary to prevent the items from being hidden, lost, damaged, changed or destroyed.

255.   Under *paragraph 5(2)*, the power in paragraph 3(4) to inspect and take copies of documents includes power to require information stored in electronic form on the premises, or accessible from the premises, to be produced in a form which can be taken away and which enables it to be read or easily changed into a readable format. This would include for example printing copies of electronic documents or downloading copies of files from a computer so that they can be printed at a later date.

256.   *Paragraph 5(3)* of Schedule 5 makes clear that the person exercising the power under paragraph 3 may not seize items which they believe to be subject to legal privilege.

257.   Under *paragraph 5(4) and (5)*, items seized or taken away under paragraph 3 may be kept for as long as they are needed, and reasonable force may be used in the exercising of the power.

Paragraph 6: Exhumation of body for examination
258.   *Paragraph 6* of Schedule 5 sets out the powers of a senior coroner to order the exhumation of a body. This paragraph, to a great extent, replicates section 23 of the 1988 Act.

259.   *Paragraph 6(2)* enables a senior coroner to order the exhumation of the body of a person buried in England and Wales if the senior coroner thinks it is necessary for a post-mortem examination to be made of the body. Although a senior coroner may order the exhumation of a body buried anywhere in England and Wales, it is likely that a senior coroner will only order the exhumation of a body if it is within that coroner's area. This is because the senior coroner will only have jurisdiction to investigate the death due to the initial presence of the body within his or her area. The exceptions to this are where another senior coroner has been asked to conduct an investigation under section 2; the Chief Coroner

has directed another senior coroner to conduct an investigation under section 3 or a fresh investigation is ordered after an appeal. A coroner will in all cases have power to order the exhumation of a body for purposes of a post-mortem examination under section 14 even if the body is not within his or her area.

260.   *Paragraph 6(3)* enables a senior coroner to order exhumation of a body buried within his or her coroner area if the senior coroner thinks it necessary for the body to be examined for the purpose of any criminal proceedings or possible criminal proceedings in respect of the death of that person or another person who died in circumstances connected to that person's death.

Paragraph 7: Action to prevent other deaths
261.   *Paragraph 7* of Schedule 5 gives the senior coroner the power, at the end of an investigation, to report the matter to authorities or organisations with a view to preventing deaths in the future. This power could, for example, be used by the senior coroner to report to a local authority the fact that several deaths have occurred in similar circumstances on the same stretch of road. The person or organisation to whom the report was made must respond in writing to that report. Further provision may be made in regulations enabling reports and responses to be published.

262.   All reports made under this paragraph, and all responses to them, must be copied to the Chief Coroner, and summarised in the Chief Coroner's annual report to the Lord Chancellor (see section 36(4)(d)).

Section 33 and Schedule 6: Offences
263.   This section gives effect to Schedule 6 which sets out offences relating to jurors, witnesses and evidence, and the penalties for these offences.

264.   Offences relating to jurors include service on a jury by those who know they are disqualified from such service, failure to attend a coroner's jury and making false representations to avoid jury service. These offences reflect those jury-related offences in section 9 of the 1988 Act.

265.   The offences relating to witnesses include failure to comply with a notice under paragraph 1 of Schedule 5, altering evidence, preventing evidence from being given, destroying or concealing documents, and giving false evidence. These offences are new, as the senior coroner is given the power to compel evidence in these provisions.

266.   The Act does not remove or alter the powers of a senior coroner under the common law to summon witnesses, require evidence to be given and punish for contempt of court.

Section 34 and Schedule 7: Allowances, fees and expenses
267.   This section gives effect to Schedule 7 which gives the Lord Chancellor regulation-making powers regarding fees and allowances that the senior coroner can pay (or are paid on his or her behalf, for example by the local authority) to jurors and witnesses to cover costs incurred due to their attendance at an inquest or pre-inquest hearing. This Schedule also

provides for other payments to be made by senior coroners to practitioners who conduct post-mortem examinations. It allows senior coroners to charge for supplying copies of documents. A relevant authority can issue a schedule of the fees, allowances and other payments that senior coroners can make.

268.   The Schedule also provides for coroners, the Chief Coroner, Deputy Chief Coroner, Coroner for Treasure, or a judge, former judge or former coroner, when carrying out an investigation, to be indemnified, or reimbursed any costs, in connection with: costs arising from legal claims made in relation to exercise of the person's powers or functions; disputes of claims as to what they may, or may not have done; damages awarded against them; or in costs ordered to be paid by them in connection with such proceedings. This replicates the effect of Section 27A of the 1988 Act which required a council to indemnify a coroner for expenses reasonably incurred in connection with his or her functions, or in relation to disputing a claim made against him or her.

269.   Section 27 of the 1988 Act required senior coroners to produce accounts to the council of their appointing local authority, and made provision as to the funds from which reimbursements should be paid. Provision about such matters will now be contained in secondary legislation.

Chapter 6: Governance etc

Section 35 and Schedule 8: Chief Coroner and Deputy Chief Coroners
270.   The Act creates the offices of Chief Coroner and Deputy Chief Coroners, who will be responsible for hearing appeals against decisions of coroners, for establishing and overseeing national performance standards, and for providing leadership to the service in general. They may also conduct investigations. The Government intends to have one full time Chief Coroner and one full time Deputy Chief Coroner, and to appoint others as Deputy Chief Coroners to assist, if required, in particular to hear appeals.

271.   Section 35 also gives effect to Schedule 8, which makes provision for the appointment of the Chief Coroner and Deputy Chief Coroners and their respective terms of office, and specifies further functions.

272.   Under *paragraph 1* of Schedule 8, a person has to be a High Court or Circuit judge under the age of 70 to be eligible for appointment as Chief Coroner.

273.   *Paragraph 2* of Schedule 8 sets out the eligibility criteria and appointment process for Deputy Chief Coroners; it requires appointees to be under the age of 70 and be a High Court or Circuit judge, the Coroner for Treasure or a senior coroner. It also specifies that the Lord Chief Justice will consult the Lord Chancellor as to the number of Deputy Chief Coroners that are needed, and how many of these should be judges, and how many should be senior coroners.

274.   *Paragraph 2(4)* of Schedule 8 states that the Lord Chief Justice will (after consulting the Lord Chancellor) appoint Circuit or High Court judges as Deputy Chief Coroners. By *paragraph 2(5)* the term of appointment will be decided by the Lord Chief Justice after consulting the Lord Chancellor. *Paragraph 2(6)* provides that the Lord Chancellor, at the invitation of the Lord Chief Justice, will be responsible for appointing senior coroners as Deputy Chief Coroners. The Lord Chancellor will make appointments following a Judicial Appointments Commission process and will decide the term after consulting the Lord Chief Justice.

275.   There is a retirement age of 70 for the Chief and Deputy Chief Coroners. This Schedule also sets out the arrangements for vacation of the office, resignation, removal from office and remuneration. It also provides for the Chief Coroner and Deputy Chief Coroners to be indemnified for costs they incur in connection with legal proceedings arising from the carrying out of their duties and exercise of their powers, damages awarded against them, and in costs ordered to be paid by them in connection with such proceedings.

276.   Schedule 8 also provides for a Deputy Chief Coroner to perform the functions of the Chief Coroner if the latter is absent or unavailable, the office is vacant or otherwise with the Chief Coroner's consent, and allows the Lord Chancellor to appoint staff to assist the Chief and Deputy Chief Coroners.

Section 36: Reports and advice to the Lord Chancellor from the Chief Coroner
277.   *Subsection (1)* requires the Chief Coroners to give an annual report to the Lord Chancellor.

278.   The Chief Coroner's annual report must cover any matters he or she wishes to bring to the attention of the Lord Chancellor, and any matters the Lord Chancellor has asked the Chief Coroner to cover in the report. The report must also contain an assessment of consistency of standards between coroner areas; information about investigations that have taken over 12 months to complete; authorisations given under Schedule 5 for coroners to enter and search land and seize items; the number, nature and outcomes of appeals made to the Chief Coroner; and a summary of matters reported by coroners under paragraph 7 of Schedule 5 to prevent future deaths, and the responses to those reports under sub-paragraph (2) of that paragraph.

279.   The annual report must be published by the Lord Chancellor, and a copy would be laid before each House of Parliament.

280.   As well as producing an annual report from the Chief Coroner to the Lord Chancellor, it is also intended that the Chief Coroner will be able to publish occasional summaries of the reports made by coroners to prevent future deaths and the responses to them.

281.   If requested to do so by the Lord Chancellor, the Chief Coroner must by virtue of *subsection (7)* give advice to the Lord Chancellor about particular matters relating to the operation of the coroner system.

Section 37: Regulations about training
282.   This section provides that the Chief Coroner may, with the agreement of the Lord Chancellor, make regulations about the training of all levels of coroners, coroners' officers and other staff who support coroners. This is designed to ensure that all those working within the coroners' service are aware of and apply best practice, relevant guidelines and standards issued under section 42 (for example) and other developments in legislation.

Section 38 and Schedule 9: Medical Adviser to the Chief Coroner
283.   This section and Schedule provide for the appointment of a person as Medical Adviser to the Chief Coroner (MACC), and a person (or persons) to be appointed as Deputy Medical Adviser (or Advisers) to the Chief Coroner (DMACC). These persons will be appointed formally by the Lord Chancellor, following consultation with the Chief Coroner, and Welsh Ministers, as responsibility for health matters is devolved to the Welsh Assembly Government. Terms and conditions will be set by the Lord Chancellor as he or she considers appropriate.

284.   The MACC will advise and assist the Chief Coroner in relation to medical matters which are relevant to the coroner system. The DMACC will perform the MACC's functions when the MACC is absent or unavailable or if the post is vacant; or at any other time with the MACC's consent.

285.   *Paragraph 3* of the Schedule specifies that, in order to be eligible for the role of MACC or DMACC, a person must be a registered medical practitioner and have been so throughout the previous five years, and have practised within the previous five years.

Section 39: Inspection of coroner system
286.   This section sets out that Her Majesty's Inspectorate of Courts Administration will carry out inspections of the operation of the coroner system, and report their findings to the Lord Chancellor. The Chief Coroner and Deputy Chief Coroners (or a person acting as a senior coroner under Schedule 10) will not be inspected in relation to any functions they carry out as such.

287.   Under *subsection (2)*, inspectors will not be able to inspect persons making judicial decisions or exercising judicial discretion. This would include decisions taken about whether or not to order a post-mortem examination or matters relating to the scope or conduct of inquests.

288.   Under *subsection (3),* the Chief Inspector must report to the Lord Chancellor on any matter related to the operation of the coroner system that the Lord Chancellor refers to the Chief Inspector. There is also provision (in section 60(5) of the Courts Act 2003) enabling an inspector to carry out the Chief Inspector's functions in the event that he or she is unable to do so.

289.   Under *subsection (4)*, the section provides for inspectors to enter coroners' work premises and to take copies of any relevant records. Although they will be entitled to be present at inquests, under *subsection (5)* they will not be able to attend private deliberations, such as jury meetings, or inquests where there has been a direction to exclude persons under Coroners rules (see section 45(3)).

290.   Where a report under *subsection (1)* or *(3)* recommends that action is taken by a senior coroner, there is power in *subsection (8)* for the Lord Chancellor to direct the senior coroner to take the action within a specified period.

Section 40: Appeals to the Chief Coroner
291.   This section provides a right of appeal to the Chief Coroner against decisions that fall within *subsection (2)*. This right is only open to interested persons (as defined in section 47) although *subsection (5)* enables a person who the senior coroner decides is not classed as an interested person to appeal against the decision that he or she is not an interested person. If such an appeal is upheld by the Chief Coroner, then that person would also be entitled to appeal against the decisions listed in *subsection (2)*.

292.   *Subsection (2)* sets out the decisions that can be appealed. Appeals can for example be made against a decision to conduct or not conduct an investigation, a decision to discontinue an investigation and a decision to resume or not resume an investigation, for example, once criminal proceedings or an inquiry under the Inquiries Act 2005 have concluded. It will be possible to appeal a coroner's decision not to request a post-mortem examination. A coroner's decision that a post-mortem examination is needed will not be subject to appeal however, except where a post-mortem of the same type has already been carried out. It will be possible to appeal against a decision as to whether an inquest is held with a jury.

293.   A coroner's determination as to who the deceased was, and how, when and where the deceased came by his or her death (and, where relevant, the circumstances of the death) can also be appealed, as can his or her finding of details required for registration of the death.

294.   *Subsection (3)* provides for interested persons to appeal decisions of the Coroner for Treasure (or Assistant Coroner for Treasure) in relation to treasure investigations.

295.   *Subsection (6)* enables the Lord Chancellor to change the list of decisions in subsection (2) by making an order.

296.   Rules under section 45 will set out the procedure for appeals to be made to the Chief Coroner.

297.   This route of appeal is new. Under the previous law, there was no appeal as such against a coroner's decisions. An application could be made to the High Court under section 13 of the 1988 Act if a coroner refused to hold an inquest or where a fresh inquest is required. The High Court could compel a coroner to hold an inquest or quash the determination of a previous inquest and order a fresh inquest. Persons with sufficient interest could also apply for judicial review of a coroner's decision. However, there was no simple appeal route for

bereaved people and other interested persons. This section provides a route of appeal to the Chief Coroner. It also replaces the statutory procedure of application to the High Court by giving the Chief Coroner power to compel a coroner to hold an inquest, or to amend or quash a determination or finding.

298.   *Subsection (7)* allows the Chief Coroner to consider any evidence which he or she thinks is relevant to the substance of the decision, determination or finding against which an appeal has been brought. This can include considering evidence which relates to issues that arose after the decision, determination or finding was made.

299.   If the Chief Coroner allows an appeal that is not an appeal against a finding or determination, he or she can substitute his or her own decision or quash the decision and refer it back to the senior coroner for a fresh decision. If the appeal is against a finding or determination, the Chief Coroner can amend it, or quash it and order a fresh investigation. If the appeal is against a failure to make a decision – for example, to conduct an investigation – the Chief Coroner can make the decision that could have been made or, again, refer the matter back to the senior coroner for him or her to make a decision. The Chief Coroner may also make any order he or she sees fit, including an order in relation to costs, although he or she has no authority in relation to the award of legal aid.

300.   A decision of the Chief Coroner or a Deputy Chief Coroner may be appealed to the Court of Appeal, on a point of law only. The Court of Appeal can either confirm the decision made by the Chief Coroner, substitute its own decision or quash the decision and ask the Chief Coroner to make a fresh decision.

301.   Different appeal arrangements apply when the person acting as coroner is a High Court or Circuit Judge, in which case the appeal is to the Court of Appeal or a High Court judge, respectively (see paragraph 4 of Schedule 10).

Section 41 and Schedule 10: Investigation by Chief Coroner or Coroner for Treasure or by judge, former judge or former coroner
302.   This section gives effect to Schedule 10 which provides for the arrangements when an investigation into a death is to be conducted by the Chief Coroner or the Coroner for Treasure, or by a judge, former judge or former coroner, by invitation of the Chief Coroner.

303.   The Chief Coroner can by virtue of *paragraph 1* personally conduct investigations. He or she can also arrange, with the permission of the Lord Chief Justice, for a judge (including a retired judge who has not reached the age of 70) to conduct an investigation. This will be appropriate when a case has particularly complex legal or factual characteristics, but it is envisaged that the power will be used sparingly. Arrangements can also be made for a retired or former senior coroner to conduct an investigation and this might be appropriate where backlogs have built up in a particular area or in an emergency situation.

Section 42: Guidance by the Lord Chancellor

304.   This section enables the Lord Chancellor to issue guidance about how the coroner system is expected to operate for interested persons. It is intended that the first such guidance will be in relation to bereaved people, in the form of a Charter for the Bereaved, a draft of which was published on 14 January 2009. Further non-statutory guidance may be introduced for other classes of interested persons in the future.

305.   *Subsection (4)* specifies that the Lord Chancellor must consult the Chief Coroner before issuing, changing or withdrawing any such guidance.

Chapter 7: Supplementary

Section 43: Coroners regulations

306.   This section enables the Lord Chancellor, with the agreement of the Lord Chief Justice, to make regulations for regulating the practice and procedure in connection with investigations (excluding inquests), post-mortem examinations and exhumations.

307.   Regulations will include, for example, arrangements for:

- suspending and resuming investigations;

- discharging an investigation and providing for fresh investigations;

- delegation of a senior coroner's functions relating to investigations;

- retention, release and disposal of bodies including reinterment; and

- exercise of the powers of entry, search and seizure.

Section 44: Treasure regulations

308.   Treasure regulations may be made on the same basis as those under section 43. The Lord Chancellor will make the regulations with the agreement of the Lord Chief Justice or a judicial nominee. These regulations may also apply provisions of Coroners rules (*subsection (4)*).

309.   Regulations will include, for example, arrangements for:

- delegation of the Coroner for Treasure's functions;

- requiring information to be given to the Chief Coroner for an annual report under section 36(1); and

- exercise of the powers of entry, search and seizure in relation to treasure investigations.

Section 45: Coroners rules

310. This section enables Rules to be made by the Lord Chief Justice (or his or her nominee) as to the practice and procedure at or in connection with inquests and appeals to the Chief Coroner, thus separating out the inquest component of the senior coroner's investigation. It replicates the power in section 32 of the 1988 Act.

311. *Subsection (2)* sets out particular matters about which rules can be made. These are as follows:

- Subsection (2)(a) allows for rules regarding evidence including sworn and unsworn evidence;

- Subsection (2)(b) allows for rules regarding discharging a jury and summoning a new jury;

- Subsection (2)(c) concerns discharging inquests and holding fresh inquests;

- Subsection (2)(d) concerns adjourning and resuming inquests;

- Subsection (2)(e) would allow the senior coroner to direct that a person's name should not be disclosed except to persons specified in the direction. It is anticipated that any provision made in rules for this discretion will be used sparingly, for example during inquests into the deaths of UK Special Forces personnel or other investigations where witnesses need to remain anonymous to protect their safety;

- Subsection (2)(f) provides for rules relating to a senior coroner delegating his or her non-judicial functions:

- Subsection (2)(g) permits rules about disclosure of information held by the senior coroner:

- Subsection (2)(h) concerns excusing persons from jury service;

- Subsection (2)(i) allows for rules that would clarify when the Coroner for Treasure should hold an inquest into a possible treasure find; and

- Subsection (2)(j) allows for rules requiring permission to be given to an appeal to the Court of Appeal.

312. *Subsection (3)* sets out particular matters in relation to which rules can confer a power on a senior coroner or the Coroner for Treasure. *Subsection (3)(a)* would enable the coroner to decide that, if in his or her opinion the interests of national security required it, certain persons should be excluded from attending all or part of an inquest.

313.   *Subsection (3)(b)* enables a senior coroner or the Coroner for Treasure to exclude persons from an inquest during the giving of evidence by a person aged under 18. A child or young person may find giving evidence at an inquest intimidating or traumatic. These powers would enable the coroner to be flexible about how evidence could be given.

Section 46: Abolition of the office of coroner of the Queen's household
314.   This section abolishes the office of coroner of the Queen's household. In future, any investigation which would have been carried out by the coroner of the Queen's household will be carried out by the senior coroner in whose area the body is, or by a coroner directed by the Chief Coroner to carry out the investigation or by a coroner requested to carry out the investigation under section 2.

Section 47: "Interested person"
315.   This section lists those who come within the definition of the term "interested person". "Interested persons" have, amongst other things, the right to appeal against certain decisions made during the course of investigations and inquests (section 40). In addition to the specific list of those that fall into the category of "interested person", there is power for the coroner to determine that any other person is an interested person. This expands slightly the list of "interested persons" in rule 20(2) of the 1984 Rules and is intended to capture, for example, the role of the Independent Police Complaints Commission in conducting and managing some investigations.

316.   *Subsection (6)* lists those who can be classed as an "interested person" for investigations into treasure finds.

Section 48: Interpretation: general
317.   This section explains the meaning of various terms used within this Part of the Act: for example, where the word "body" is used, this includes body parts.

Section 49 and Schedule 11: Amendments to the Coroners Act (Northern Ireland) 1959
318.   *Subsection (1)* amends section 13 of the 1959 Act to enable a coroner to hold an inquest if informed that the body of a deceased person is lying within the coroner's district, irrespective of where the death took place. This will enable inquests to take place where a death has occurred abroad and the body is returned to Northern Ireland.

319.   *Subsection (2)* introduces Schedule 11, which substitutes for section 17 of the 1959 Act new sections 17A to 17C, which make provision concerning witnesses and evidence and related offences in relation to inquests in Northern Ireland. This brings Northern Ireland into line with the reformed system in England and Wales, as it contains provisions which are broadly equivalent to those contained in Schedule 6.

Section 50: Amendments to the Fatal Accidents and Sudden Deaths Inquiry (Scotland) Act 1976

320.   This section makes amendments to the Fatal Accidents and Sudden Deaths Inquiry (Scotland) Act 1976 (the 1976 Act). *Subsection (2)* inserts a new section 1A into the 1976 Act. If subsection (4) of new section 1A applies, the procurator fiscal for the appropriate district will be required to investigate the circumstances of a death and apply to the sheriff to hold a Fatal Accident Inquiry.

321.   Subsection (4) of new section 1A will apply if three conditions are met. First, the Lord Advocate is notified under section 12 (discussed at paragraphs 124 to 130) by the Secretary of State or Chief Coroner that it may be appropriate for a death to be investigated under the 1976 Act. Secondly (in the same way that Fatal Accident Inquiries would be triggered for a death that occurs in Scotland) the person who died was either in legal custody at the time of death or the death was sudden, suspicious or unexplained or the circumstances of the death would give rise to serious public concern. And thirdly, the Lord Advocate decides that it would be appropriate for a Fatal Accident Inquiry to be held into the death and does not reverse this decision.

322.   Subsection (5) of new section 1A provides that subsection (4) does not apply to a death if the Lord Advocate is satisfied that criminal proceedings have sufficiently established the circumstances of the death.

323.   Subsection (6) of new section 1A outlines the process of an application from the procurator fiscal to the sheriff for a Fatal Accident Inquiry. Subsection (7) gives the Lord Advocate the responsibility for determining the appropriate district and sheriffdom.

324.   *Subsections (3) to (5)* make consequential amendments to sections 2, 3 and 6 of the 1976 Act.

Section 51: Public funding for advocacy at certain inquests

325.   Section 6(6) of the Access to Justice Act 1999 states that the Legal Services Commission may not fund, as part of the Community Legal Service, any of the services specified in Schedule 2 to that Act. Paragraph 2 of Schedule 2 states that the Legal Services Commission may not fund advocacy, except in the circumstances listed in that paragraph.

326.   Section 51 amends the list in paragraph 2 of circumstances where advocacy can be made available by adding (a) inquests into the deaths of British service personnel who die while on active service, and (b) inquests into the deaths of persons who die while in the custody of the State, or those who die in the course of a police action or arrest. The Legal Services Commission will be authorised to fund advocacy for family members to be represented at such inquests, subject to the funding criteria in the Funding Code made under section 8 of the Access to Justice Act 1999 being met. Funding would also be subject to a means test.

Part 2 - Criminal offences

Chapter 1: Murder, infanticide and suicide

Section 52: Persons suffering from diminished responsibility (England and Wales)
327.   The effect of section 52 is to replace the current definition of the partial defence of diminished responsibility with a modernised definition based on the concept of "an abnormality of mental functioning" arising from a "recognised medical condition". The new definition requires that the abnormality substantially impaired the defendant's ability to do one (or more) of three things and also provides that the defendant's abnormality of mental functioning should be at least a significant contributory factor in causing the defendant's acts or omissions.

328.   *Subsection (1)* replaces the current subsection (1) of section 2 of the Homicide Act 1957 (the 1957 Act) with new subsections (1) to (1B). The amended section provides that a person is not to be convicted of murder if he or she was suffering from an abnormality of mental functioning which meets the three conditions set out in new section 2(1)(a) to (c). As now, under section 2(2) of the 1957 Act, the person will be convicted of the offence of manslaughter instead of murder.

329.   New section 2(1)(a) sets out that the abnormality of mental functioning has to arise from a recognised medical condition. New section 2(1)(b) provides that the abnormality of mental functioning must have impaired the defendant's ability to do one or more of the things mentioned in new section 2(1A). These are the ability of that person to understand the nature of his or her conduct, to form a rational judgement or to exercise self-control. This contrasts with the existing definition of the partial defence which requires a person's mental responsibility to be substantially impaired but does not specify in what respects this must be so.

330.   New section 2(1)(c) sets out that, in order for the partial defence to apply, the abnormality of mental functioning must provide an explanation for the defendant's involvement in the killing. New section 2(1B) clarifies that this will be the case where the abnormality was at least a significant contributory factor in causing the defendant to carry out the conduct.

331.   *Subsection (2)* updates the language of section 6 of the Criminal Procedure (Insanity) Act 1964 insofar as it refers to the partial defence of diminished responsibility.

Section 53: Persons suffering from diminished responsibility (Northern Ireland)
332.   This section makes provision for Northern Ireland equivalent to section 52.

Section 54: Partial defence to murder: loss of control
333.   Provocation is a common law partial defence supplemented by section 3 of the 1957 Act. Under the partial defence, a defendant who would otherwise be guilty of murder will be guilty of manslaughter instead if he or she was provoked by things said or done (or both) to lose self-control, and in the opinion of the jury the provocation was enough to make a reasonable person do as the defendant did.

334.   Section 56 abolishes the common law partial defence of provocation and replaces it with a new partial defence to murder of "loss of control" at sections 54 and 55.

335.   Section 54 sets out the criteria which need to be met in order for the new partial defence of loss of self-control to be successful.

336.   *Subsection (1)* lists those as:

a)   the defendant's conduct resulted from a loss of self-control,
b)   the loss of self-control had a qualifying trigger (which is defined in section 55), and
c)   a person of the defendant's sex and age with an ordinary level of tolerance and self-restraint and in the circumstances of the defendant might have acted in the same or similar way to the defendant.

337.   *Subsection (2)* clarifies that the loss of control described in subsection (1) need not be sudden. Under the existing common law partial defence of provocation, the courts have held that the loss of self-control must be sudden. Case law has developed over time to the effect that the partial defence might still apply though where there was a delay between the provocative incident and the killing. The length of time between the incident and the killing does however affect whether there is sufficient evidence of a loss of self-control for the judge to leave the issue to the jury, and how readily a jury accepts that the defendant had indeed lost his or her self-control at the time of the killing. Although subsection (2) in the new partial defence makes clear that it is not a requirement for the new partial defence that the loss of self control be sudden, it will remain open, as at present, for the judge (in deciding whether to leave the defence to the jury) and the jury (in determining whether the killing did in fact result from a loss of self-control and whether the other aspects of the partial defence are satisfied) to take into account any delay between a relevant incident and the killing.

338.   *Subsection (3)* supplements subsection (1)(c) by clarifying that the reference to the defendant's circumstances in that subsection means all of those circumstances except those whose only relevance to the defendant's conduct is that they impact upon the defendant's general level of tolerance and self-restraint. Thus, a defendant's history of abuse at the hands of the victim could be taken into account in deciding whether an ordinary person might have acted as the defendant did, whereas the defendant's generally short temper could not. Consequently, when applying the test in subsection (1)(c) the jury will consider whether a person of the defendant's sex and age with an ordinary level of tolerance and self-restraint and in the defendant's specific circumstances (in the sense described earlier in this paragraph) might have acted as the defendant did.

339.   *Subsection (4)* ensures that those acting in a considered desire for revenge cannot rely on the partial defence, even if they lose self-control as a result of a qualifying trigger.

340.   *Subsection (5)* clarifies where the burden of proof lies in murder cases where the partial defence is raised. If sufficient evidence of the partial defence is raised, the burden of disproving the defence beyond reasonable doubt rests with the prosecution.   It is supplemented by *subsection (6)* which confirms that for the purposes of subsection (5) the evidence will be sufficient to raise an issue as to the defence where a jury, properly directed, could reasonably conclude that the partial defence might apply. It will be a matter of law, and therefore for a judge to decide, whether sufficient evidence has been raised to leave the partial defence to the jury. This differs from the position with the existing partial defence of provocation where, if there is evidence that a person was provoked to lose his or her self-control, the judge is required by section 3 of the 1957 Act to leave the partial defence to the jury even where no jury could reasonably conclude that a reasonable person would have reacted as the defendant did. Where there is sufficient evidence for the issue to be considered by the jury, the burden will be on the prosecution to disprove it. This is the same burden of proof as other defences, including self-defence.

341.   *Subsection (7)* sets out that, when the defence is successful, the defendant will be guilty of manslaughter instead of murder.

342.   *Subsection (8)* provides that even if one party to a killing is found not guilty of murder on the grounds of the partial defence of loss of self control, this does not affect the position of any other person who may be liable for murder in respect of the killing.

Section 55: Meaning of "qualifying trigger"
343.   Section 55 defines the term "qualifying trigger" for purposes of section 54. Under section 54 (1)(b) the loss of self-control must have a qualifying trigger in order for the partial defence to apply.

344.   *Subsections (2) to (5)* set out that the qualifying triggers for a loss of self-control are where the loss of self-control was attributable to a fear of serious violence, to certain things done or said (or both) or to a combination of both of these.

345.   Subsection (3) deals with cases where the defendant lost self-control because of his or her fear of serious violence from the victim. As in the complete defence of self-defence, this will be a subjective test and the defendant will need to show that he or she lost self-control because of a genuine fear of serious violence, whether or not the fear was in fact reasonable. The fear of serious violence needs to be in respect of violence against the defendant or against another identified person. For example, the fear of serious violence could be in respect of a child or other relative of the defendant, but it could not be a fear that the victim would in the future use serious violence against people generally.

346.   Subsection (4) sets out when a thing or things done or said (or both) can amount to a qualifying trigger for the loss of self-control. The thing(s) done or said must amount to circumstances of an extremely grave character and cause the defendant to have a justifiable sense of being seriously wronged. Whether a defendant's sense of being seriously wronged is justifiable will be an objective question for a jury to determine (assuming that there is sufficient evidence for the defence to be left to the jury).

347.   Subsection (4) therefore sets a very high threshold for the circumstances in which a partial defence is available where a person loses self-control in response to words or actions. The effect is to substantially narrow the potential availability of a partial defence in cases where a loss of control is attributable to things done or said compared to the current partial defence of provocation (where no threshold exists in relation to the provoking circumstances).

348.   Subsection (5) allows the loss of self-control to be triggered by a combination of a fear of serious violence and a thing or things done or said which constitute circumstances of an extremely grave character and cause the defendant to have a justifiable sense of being seriously wronged.

349.   *Subsection (6)* makes further provision in relation to determining whether a loss of self-control has a qualifying trigger:

- Subsection (6)(a) provides that, when the defendant's fear of serious violence was caused by something that the defendant incited for the purpose of providing an excuse to use violence, it is to be disregarded. The effect is that, in such a situation, the person would not be able to claim a partial defence based on his or her fear of serious violence as referred to in section 55(3).

- Subsection (6)(b) provides that, when the defendant's sense of being seriously wronged by a thing done or said relates to something that the defendant incited for the purpose of providing an excuse to use violence, the sense of being seriously wronged is not justifiable. The effect is that, in such a situation, the person would not be able to claim a partial defence based on the relevant things done or said as referred to in section 55(4).

- Subsection (6)(c) provides that, in determining whether a loss of self-control has a qualifying trigger, the fact that a thing done or said amounted to sexual infidelity is to be disregarded. So, if a thing done or said, as referred to in section 55(4), amounts to sexual infidelity, that fact is disregarded in determining whether the qualifying trigger in section 55(4) applies. The effect is that, if a person kills another because they have been unfaithful, he or she will not be able to claim the partial defence. It is the fact of sexual infidelity that falls to be disregarded under the provision, so the thing done or said can still potentially amount to a qualifying trigger if (ignoring the sexual infidelity) it amounts nonetheless to circumstances of an extremely grave character causing the defendant to have a justifiable sense of being seriously wronged. This may arise only rarely, but an example of where it might be relevant is where a person discovers their partner sexually abusing their young child (an act that amounts to sexual infidelity) and loses self-control and kills. The fact that the partner's act amounted to sexual infidelity must be discounted but that act may still potentially be claimed to amount to the qualifying trigger in section 55(4) on the basis of the other aspects of the case (namely the child abuse).

Section 56: Abolition of common law defence of provocation

350.   Section 56 abolishes the common law defence of provocation, and consequently repeals section 3 of 1957 Act and the equivalent Northern Ireland provision, namely section 7 of the Criminal Justice Act (Northern Ireland) 1966.   Section 3 supplemented the common law principles relating to provocation by providing that the issue of whether the provocation was enough to make a reasonable person do as the defendant did should be left to be determined by the jury. This has been interpreted as meaning that a judge must leave the partial defence to the jury even where the evidence is such that no jury properly directed could reasonably conclude that a reasonable person would have reacted as the defendant did. This is in contrast to the common law position that existed prior to the Homicide Act 1957, where the judge was not required to leave the issue to the jury in such circumstances.

Section 57: Infanticide (England and Wales)

351.   Section 57 amends section 1 of the Infanticide Act 1938 so that it is clear that the offence and defence of infanticide are available only in respect of a woman who would otherwise be found guilty of murder or manslaughter. Whilst it had generally been assumed in the past that infanticide could apply only in circumstances that would otherwise amount to the offence of murder, the Court of Appeal ruled in *R v Gore* [2007] EWCA Crim 2789 that section 1 may apply whenever the requirements of infanticide are made out regardless of what offence would otherwise have been committed.

352.   Section 57 limits infanticide to cases that would otherwise be murder or manslaughter through two changes. The first is to replace the words "notwithstanding that" with the word "if". This resolves an uncertainty that has existed in the past about the meaning of the term "notwithstanding that" which at different times has been interpreted as meaning "even if" and "provided that".

353.   The second is to explicitly state that infanticide can apply (provided all the other criteria for infanticide apply) where the offence would otherwise be murder *or manslaughter.*

354.   The combined effect of the two changes is that infanticide can apply "if the circumstances were such that but for the Infanticide Act 1938 the offence would have amounted to murder or manslaughter".

Section 58: Infanticide (Northern Ireland)

355.   This section makes provision for Northern Ireland equivalent to section 57.

Section 59: Encouraging or assisting suicide: England and Wales

356.   Section 2(1) of the Suicide Act 1961 provides that a person who "aids, abets, counsels or procures" the suicide or attempted suicide of another person commits an offence (the substantive offence).   By virtue of section 1 of the Criminal Attempts Act 1981 it is also an offence to attempt to aid, abet, counsel or procure the suicide or attempted suicide of another person (the attempt offence).   Section 59 replaces the substantive and attempt offences with a single offence expressed in terms of "encouraging or assisting" the suicide or attempted suicide of another person. Paragraph 58 of Schedule 21 therefore disapplies the Criminal Attempts Act 1981 in respect of an offence under section 2 of the Suicide Act 1961. The section simplifies and modernises the law with the aim of improving understanding of this

area of the law. It is in line with the case law relating to the existing substantive and attempt offences. The section does not change the scope of the current law, when section 2 of the Suicide Act 1961 is read in combination with section 1 of the Criminal Attempts Act 1981.

357.   *Subsection (2)* replaces section 2(1) of the Suicide Act 1961. It provides that a person commits an offence if he or she does an act which is capable of encouraging or assisting another person to commit or attempt to commit suicide, and if he or she intends the act to encourage or assist another person to commit or attempt to commit suicide. The person committing the offence need not know, or even be able to identify, the other person. So, for example, the author of a website promoting suicide who intends that one or more of his or her readers will commit or attempt to commit suicide is guilty of an offence, even though he or she may never know the identity of those who access the website. The offence applies whether or not a person commits or attempts suicide.

358.   *Subsection (3)* amends section 2(2) of the Suicide Act 1961 so that the language is consistent with the new section 2(1).

359.   *Subsection (4)* inserts new sections 2A and 2B into the Suicide Act 1961. The new section 2A elaborates on what constitutes an act capable of encouraging or assisting suicide. New section 2A(1) provides that a person who arranges for someone else to do an act capable of encouraging or assisting the suicide or attempted suicide of another person will be liable for the offence if the other person does that act. New section 2A(2) has the effect that an act can be capable of encouraging or assisting suicide even if the circumstances are such that it was impossible for the act to actually encourage or assist suicide. An act is therefore treated as capable of encouraging and assisting suicide if it would have been so capable had the facts been as the defendant believed them to be at the time of the act (for example, if pills provided with the intention that they will assist a person to commit suicide are thought to be lethal but are in fact harmless) or had subsequent events happened as the defendant believed they would (for example, if lethal pills which were sent to a person with the intention that the person would use them to commit or attempt to commit suicide get lost in the post), or both. New section 2A(3) clarifies that references to doing an act capable of encouraging or assisting another to commit or attempt suicide include a reference to doing so by threatening another person or otherwise putting pressure on another person to commit or attempt suicide. The new section 2B provides that an act includes a course of conduct.

Section 60: Encouraging or assisting suicide (Northern Ireland)
360.   This section makes provision for Northern Ireland equivalent to section 59.

Section 61 and Schedule 12: Encouraging or assisting suicide: providers of information society services
361.   Section 61 and Schedule 12 ensure that the provisions outlined in sections 59 and 60 above are consistent with the UK's obligations under the E-Commerce Directive.

362. Schedule 12 ensures that providers of information society services who are established in England, Wales or Northern Ireland are covered by the offence of encouraging or assisting suicide even when they are operating in other European Economic Area states. *Paragraphs 4 to 6* of the Schedule provide exemptions for internet service providers from the offence in limited circumstances, such as where they are acting as mere conduits for information that is capable, and provided with the intention, of encouraging or assisting suicide or are storing it as caches or hosts.

Chapter 2: Images of children

Section 62: Possession of prohibited images of children
363. *Subsection (1)* creates a new offence in England and Wales and Northern Ireland of possession of a prohibited image of a child.

364. *Subsections (2) to (8)* set out the definition of a "prohibited image of a child". Under subsection (2), in order to be a prohibited image, an image must be pornographic, fall within subsection (6) and be grossly offensive, disgusting or otherwise of an obscene character. The definition of "pornographic" is set out in subsection (3). An image must be of such a nature that it must reasonably be assumed to have been produced solely or mainly for the purpose of sexual arousal. Whether this threshold has been met will be an issue for a jury to determine. Subsection (4) makes it clear that where (as found in a person's possession) an individual image forms part of a series of images, the question of whether it is pornographic must be determined by reference both to the image itself and the context in which it appears in the series of images.

365. Subsection (5) expands on subsection (4). It provides that, where an image is integral to a narrative (for example a mainstream or documentary film) which when it is taken as a whole could not reasonably be assumed to be pornographic, the image itself may not be pornographic, even though if considered in isolation the contrary conclusion might have been reached.

366. Subsection (6) and (7) provide that a prohibited image for the purposes of the offence is one which focuses solely or principally on a child's genitals or anal region or portrays any of a list of acts set out in subsection (7).

367. Subsection (8) provides that for the purposes of subsection (7) penetration is a continuing act from entry to withdrawal.

368. *Subsection (9)* requires proceedings to be instituted by or with the consent of the Director of Public Prosecutions.

Section 63: Exclusion of classified film, etc

369.   This section provides an exclusion from the scope of the offence under section 62 for excluded images.

370.   An "excluded image" is defined in *subsection (2)* as an image which forms part of a series of images contained in a recording of the whole or part of a classified work. A "recording" is defined in *subsection (7)* as any disc, tape or other device capable of storing data electronically and from which images may be produced. This therefore includes images held on a computer. A classified work is a video work in respect of which a classification certificate has been issued by an authority designated under section 4 of the Video Recordings Act 1984.

371.   The effect of the exclusion is that a person who has a video recording of a film which has been classified by the British Board of Film Classification (BBFC), and which contains images that, despite their context, might amount to a "prohibited image of a child" for the purposes of the section 62 offence, will not be liable for prosecution for the offence.

372.   However, the effect of *subsection (3)* is that the exclusion from the scope of the offence does not apply in respect of images contained within extracts from classified films which must reasonably be assumed to have been extracted solely or principally for the purpose of sexual arousal. Essentially the exemption for an image forming part of a classified work is lost where the image is extracted from that work for pornographic purposes. Subsection (7) defines "extract" to include a single image.

373.   *Subsection (4)* provides that when an extracted image is one of a series of images, in establishing whether or not it is of such a nature that it must reasonably be assumed to have been extracted for the purpose of sexual arousal, regard is to be had to the image itself and to the context it which it appears in the series of images. This is the same test as set out in subsection (4) of section 62. Subsection (5) of section 62 also applies in determining this question.

374.   The effect of *subsection (5)* is that, in determining whether a recording is a recording of a whole or part of a classified work, alterations due to technical reasons (such as a failure in the recording system), due to inadvertence (such as setting the wrong time for a recording) or due to the inclusion of extraneous material (such as advertisements), are to be disregarded.

375.   *Subsection (6)* makes it clear that nothing in section 63 affects any duty of a designated authority to take into account the offence in section 62 when considering whether to issue a classification certificate in respect of a video work.

376.   *Subsection (7)* sets out the definitions used in this section. *Subsection (8)* states that section 22(3) of the Video Recordings Act 1984 applies. The effect of section 22(3) is that, where an alteration is made to a video work in respect of which a classification certificate has been issued, the classification certificate does not apply to the altered work.

Section 64: Defences
377. This section sets out a series of defences to the section 62 offence of possession of prohibited images of children. These defences are set out in *subsection (1)*. They are the same as those for the offence of possession of indecent images of children under section 160(2) of the Criminal Justice Act 1988 and Article 15(2) of the Criminal Justice (Evidence etc) (Northern Ireland) Order 1988. They are:

- that the person had a legitimate reason for being in possession of the image (this will cover those who can demonstrate that their legitimate business means that they have a reason for possessing the image);

- that the person had not seen the image and did not know, or have reasonable cause to suspect, that the images held were prohibited images of children (this will cover those who are in possession of offending images but are unaware of the nature of the images); and

- that the person had not asked for the image – it having been sent without request – and that he or she had not kept it for an unreasonable period of time (this will cover those who are sent unsolicited material and who act quickly to delete it or otherwise get rid of it).

378. *Subsection (2)* provides that "prohibited image" in this section has the same meaning as in section 62.

Section 65: Meaning of "image" and "child"
379. This section defines "image" and "child" for the purposes of sections 62, 63 and 64. These definitions are applied to these sections by *subsection (1)*.

380. *Subsection (2)* sets out the definition of an image. It states that for the purposes of this offence, "an image" includes still images such as photographs, or moving images such as those in a film. The term "image" also incorporates any type of data, including that stored electronically (as on a computer disk), which is capable of conversion into an image. This covers material available on computers, mobile phones or any other electronic device.

381. *Subsection (3)* provides that "image" does not include an indecent photograph or indecent pseudo-photograph of a child, as these are subject to other controls. *Subsection (4)* defines "indecent photograph" and "indecent pseudo-photograph" in accordance with the Protection of Children Act 1978 and for Northern Ireland, the Protection of Children (Northern Ireland) Order 1978. "Indecent photograph" includes an indecent film, a copy of a photograph or film, a negative and electronic data capable of conversion into a photograph. It also includes a tracing or other image derived from the whole or part of a photograph or pseudo-photograph and electronic data capable of conversion into such an image. A pseudo-photograph is an image, whether made by computer-graphics or otherwise, which appears to be a photograph and includes a copy of a pseudo-photograph and electronic data capable of conversion into a pseudo-photograph.

382.   *Subsection (5)* defines a child to be a person under 18 years of age.

383.   *Subsection (6)* requires that a person in an image is to be treated as a child if the impression conveyed by the image is that the person shown is a child, or the predominant impression conveyed is that the person shown is a child despite the fact that some of the physical characteristics shown are not of a child.

384.   *Subsection (7)* provides that references to an image of a person include references to an imaginary person, and *subsection (8)* makes it clear that references to an image of a child include references to an imaginary child.

Section 66: Penalties
385.   The penalties that will apply to persons found guilty of an offence under section 62 are set out in this section.

386.   In England and Wales and Northern Ireland on conviction on indictment the maximum sentence is imprisonment for three years.

387.   The maximum sentence on summary conviction of the offence in England and Wales is six months' imprisonment. On the commencement of section 154(1) of the 2003 Act, the maximum sentence on summary conviction in England and Wales will rise to 12 months (see paragraph 12(1) of Schedule 22 to the Act). The maximum custodial penalty on summary conviction in Northern Ireland is six months.

Section 67: Entry, search, seizure and forfeiture
388.   *Subsection (1)* applies the entry, search, seizure and forfeiture powers of the Protection of Children Act 1978 to prohibited images of children. *Subsection (2)* applies the equivalent Northern Ireland legislation.

389.   *Subsection (3)* applies these powers to prohibited images to which section 62 applies.

390.   Paragraph 12(2) of Schedule 22 to the Act provides that these powers of forfeiture have effect regardless of when the images were lawfully seized.

Section 68 and Schedule 13: Special rules relating to providers of information society services
391.   Section 68 and Schedule 13 ensure that the provisions outlined above which make it an offence to possess prohibited images of children are consistent with the UK's obligations under the E-Commerce Directive.

392.   Under Schedule 13 providers of information society services who are established in England, Wales or Northern Ireland are covered by the new offence even when they are operating in other European Economic Area states. Paragraphs 3 to 5 of the Schedule provide exemptions for internet service providers from the offence of possession of prohibited images of children in limited circumstances, such as where they are acting as mere conduits for such material or are storing it as caches or hosts.

Section 69: Indecent pseudo-photographs of children: marriage etc

393.   *Subsection (1)* amends section 1A of the Protection of Children Act 1978 to extend the "marriage and other relationships" defence to offences under that Act so that it applies in relation to "pseudo-photographs". The defence already applies to an offence under section 1(1)(a) of the Protection of Children Act 1978 of taking or making an indecent photograph of a child and to an offence under section 1(1)(b) or (c) of that Act relating to possession and distribution of an indecent photograph of a child.

394.   *Subsection (2)* amends section 160A of the Criminal Justice Act 1988 to extend the "marriage and other relationships" defence to offences under that Act to "pseudo-photographs". The defence already applies to an offence under section 160 of the Criminal Justice Act 1988 relating to possessing an indecent photograph of a child.

395.   *Subsection (3)* amends Article 15A of the Criminal Justice (Evidence etc.) (Northern Ireland) Order 1988 (SI 1988/1847 (NI.17)) to extend the "marriage and other relationships" defence to offences under that Order to "pseudo-photographs". The defence already applies to an offence under Article 15 of the Criminal Justice (Evidence etc.) (Northern Ireland) Order 1988 (SI 1988/1847 (NI 17)) relating to possession of an indecent photograph of a child.

396.   *Subsection (4)* amends Article 3B of the Protection of Children (Northern Ireland) Order 1978 (SI 1978/1047 (NI 17)) to extend to the "marriage and other relationships" defence to offences under that Order to "pseudo-photographs". The defence already applies to an offence under Article 3(1)(a) of the Protection of Children (Northern Ireland) Order 1978 (SI 1978/1047 (NI 17)) of taking or making an indecent photograph of a child and to Article 3(1)(b) or (c) of that Order relating to possession and distribution of an indecent photograph of a child.

Chapter 3: Other offences

Section 70: Genocide, crimes against humanity and war crimes

397.   Section 70 makes amendments to Part 5 of the 2001 Act in respect of the offences of genocide, crimes against humanity and war crimes. The amendments extend to England and Wales and Northern Ireland.

398.   *Subsection (3)* inserts a new section 65A into the 2001 Act. The new section makes provision for the retrospective application of the offences of genocide, crimes against humanity and war crimes and related offences to things done on or after 1st January 1991.

399.   Subsections (1), (3), (4), (5) and (7) of new section 65A have the effect of applying certain offences to acts committed on or after 1 January 1991. Those offences are genocide, crimes against humanity, war crimes, conduct ancillary to such offences committed outside the jurisdiction, offences ancillary to those offences and offences based on the responsibility of commanders and other superiors for such offences. With the exception of genocide and some of the categories of war crimes, the retrospective application of these offences is subject to a requirement that, at the time of its commission, the act constituting the offence amounted in the circumstances to a criminal offence under international law.

400.   The effect of this requirement is to allow the courts to apply these offences in the 2001 Act to the extent that they were recognised in international law during the relevant period. So, for example, if a particular offence was recognised in international law at the time of the relevant conduct but in a narrower form than that of the offence set out in the 2001 Act, the defendant may still be convicted of the offence provided that his or her conduct met the elements of the offence as recognised at the relevant time in international law. The international law requirement ensures that the provisions comply with the principles enshrined in Article 7 of the ECHR. The requirement does not apply to genocide and certain categories of war crimes as it is beyond dispute that those offences (and all their constituent elements) were fully recognised in international law in 1991. The requirement is necessary for the other offences as, whilst the vast majority of them were recognised in international law during the relevant period, a small number may have been recognised in a narrower form than that provided for in the 2001 Act and a very small number of offences may not have been sufficiently recognised at all. In addition, international law developed during the period in question.

401.   Subsection (3) also inserts a new section 65B into Part 5 of the 2001 Act. The new section modifies the penalties applicable to the offences for the period of retrospection (1 January 1991 to 1 September 2001) in respect of certain specific offences. The 2001 Act provides for a maximum sentence of 30 years' imprisonment (other than where murder is involved). The same will generally apply for offences committed from 1 January 1991. However for domestic genocide and grave breaches of the Geneva Conventions (a category of war crimes), both of which were already offences in domestic law in 1991, a maximum penalty of 14 years' imprisonment applies instead of 30 years' (other than where murder is involved). This provision ensures that a higher penalty cannot be imposed for such offences than existed in domestic law at the time of their commission and consequently ensures compliance with Article 7 of the ECHR.

402.   *Subsection (4)* inserts a new section 67A into Part 5 of the 2001 Act to make supplemental provision about UK residents. Such residents are liable under the 2001 Act for offences committed abroad if they are resident at the time of committing the crime or subsequently become resident. New section 67A makes additional provision in respect of UK residents in two ways. First, subsection (1) lists a number of categories of person who are to be treated as being resident in the UK for the specific purposes of Part 5 of the 2001 Act to the extent this would not otherwise be the case. The specific categories are listed in paragraphs (a) to (j). Secondly, subsection (2) of new section 67A provides a non-exhaustive list of considerations a court must take into account in determining whether a person is resident in the UK.

Section 71: Slavery, servitude and forced or compulsory labour
403.   Section 71 creates a new offence in England and Wales and Northern Ireland of holding someone in slavery or servitude, or requiring a person to perform forced or compulsory labour. *Subsection (1)* creates the new offence.

404.   *Subsection (2)* requires subsection (1) to be interpreted in accordance with Article 4 of the ECHR. Article 4 of the ECHR states:

"1   No one shall be held in slavery or servitude.

2   No one shall be required to perform forced or compulsory labour.

3   For the purpose of this Article the term "forced or compulsory labour" shall not include:

(a)   any work required to be done in the ordinary course of detention imposed according to the provisions of Article 5 of this Convention or during conditional release from such detention;

(b)   any service of a military character or, in case of conscientious objectors in countries where they are recognised, service exacted instead of compulsory military service;

(c)   any service exacted in case of an emergency or calamity threatening the life or well-being of the community;

(d)   any work or service which forms part of normal civic obligations."

405.   In England and Wales and Northern Ireland on conviction on indictment the maximum sentence for the new offence is imprisonment for 14 years.

406.   The maximum sentence on summary conviction for the offence in England and Wales is six months' imprisonment. On the commencement of section 154(1) of the 2003 Act, the maximum sentence on summary conviction in England and Wales will rise to 12 months. The maximum custodial penalty on summary conviction in Northern Ireland is six months.

Section 72: Conspiracy
407.   Section 72 amends section 1A of the Criminal Law Act 1977 which sets out the conditions for the offence of "conspiracy to commit offences outside the United Kingdom". As a result section 1A will apply to conspiracies to commit offences "outside England and Wales", thereby including conspiracies to commit offences in Scotland or Northern Ireland (which are not currently covered by section 1A).

408.   This change is achieved by widening the scope of the first condition in section 1A(2) of the Criminal Law Act 1977, which currently applies only to agreements to pursue a course of conduct that would involve an act or event intended to take place in a country or territory outside the United Kingdom. This condition will now be satisfied where the act or event is intended to take place outside England and Wales and therefore will include acts or events in Scotland or Northern Ireland.

409.   The section also substitutes three new subsections for section 1A(14) of the Criminal Law Act 1977. These ensure that the changes made by section 72 do not have retrospective effect. Any agreement entered into during the period beginning on 4 September 1998 and ending with the date that section 72(1) comes into force will be subject to the current wording of section 1A(2).

410.   *Subsection (2)* makes equivalent changes for Northern Ireland.

Section 73: Abolition of common law libel offences etc
411.   Section 73 abolishes the common law offences of sedition, seditious libel, defamatory libel and obscene libel in England and Wales and Northern Ireland.

Part 3 - Criminal evidence, investigations and procedure

Chapter 1: Anonymity in investigations

Section 74: Qualifying offences
412.   *Subsection (1)* stipulates that an offence is a qualifying offence if it is listed in *subsection (2)* and the condition in *subsection (3)* is satisfied in relation to it. The offences listed in subsection (2) are murder and manslaughter, and the condition in subsection (3) is that the death was caused by being shot with a firearm, and/or by being injured with a knife. The purpose of defining qualifying offence in this way is to limit investigation anonymity orders so that they are available only in respect of investigations concerning suspected homicides (murder and manslaughter) where death was caused by a gun and/or a knife.

413.   *Subsection (4)* gives power to the Secretary of State to amend subsections (2) and (3) by order so as to alter what is a qualifying offence. The order making power is subject to the affirmative resolution procedure (see section 176(4)(a) and (5)(c)).

Section 75: Qualifying criminal investigations
414.   *Subsection (1)* defines a qualifying criminal investigation as one which is conducted by an investigating authority, wholly or in part with a view to ascertaining whether a person should be charged with a qualifying offence (as defined in section 74), or whether a person charged with a qualifying offence is guilty of it. Investigating authorities are listed in *subsection (2)*. They are:

- police forces in England and Wales;

- the British Transport Police Force;

- the Serious Organised Crime Agency; and

- the Police Service of Northern Ireland.

415.   *Subsection (3)* gives power to the Secretary of State to amend *subsection (2)* by order so as to alter the list of investigating authorities. The power is linked to (although not contingent upon) the power to amend section 74. If that power is exercised so as to add a new offence to subsection (2) of that section, the power in section 75, may need to be exercised to add a person not already listed in subsection (2) as an investigating authority, if that person has power to investigate the newly added offence. This order making power is subject to the affirmative resolution procedure (see section 176(4)(a) and (5)(c)).

416.   *Subsection (4)* provides that an order made under subsection (3) may modify any provision of this Chapter.

Section 76: Investigation anonymity orders
417.   *Subsection (1)* defines an investigation anonymity order. An investigation anonymity order is an order made by a justice of the peace, in relation to a person specified in the order, prohibiting the disclosure of any information that (a) identifies the specified person as a person who is or was able or willing to assist a qualifying criminal investigation specified in the order, or (b) that might enable the specified person to be identified as such a person. The order applies to the officers and others involved in the investigation, and indeed to anybody else, including the specified person. The purpose of the order is to prevent disclosure of information relating to the identity of an individual who is or was able or willing to assist a qualifying criminal investigation, and thus to protect an informant from harm and to provide reassurance to a reluctant informant that his or her identity will be protected by a court order.

418.   *Subsection (3)* provides that an investigation anonymity order is not contravened if a person discloses information identifying the specified person, or which might enable the specified person to be identified, as someone who is or was able or willing to assist a specified qualifying criminal investigation, if the person disclosing the information does not know and has no reason to suspect that an order is in force.

419.   *Subsection (4)* provides that an investigation anonymity order is not contravened if a person discloses information which might enable the specified person to be identified as someone who is or was able or willing to assist a specified qualifying criminal investigation, if the person disclosing the information does not know, and has no reason to suspect, that the information might enable the specified person to be so identified.

420.   *Subsections (5) and (6)* provide that an investigation anonymity order is not contravened if a person ("A") discloses the fact that an investigation anonymity order has been made to another person ("B"), where A knows that B is aware that the informant for whose benefit the order was made is or was able or willing to help with an investigation.

421.   *Subsection (7)* provides that an investigation anonymity order is not contravened where disclosure of information is to a person who is involved in the specified qualifying criminal investigation or in the prosecution of an offence to which the investigation relates, and the disclosure is made for the purposes of the investigation or prosecution.

422.   *Subsection (8)* provides that an investigation anonymity order is not contravened where disclosure is required by any enactment or rule of law, or where required by a court order. However, *subsection (9)* provides that a person may not rely on subsection (8) in a case where (a) it might have been determined that the person was required or permitted to withhold the information but (b) the person disclosed the information without there having been a determination as to whether the person was required or permitted to withhold the information. The effect of subsection (9) on subsection (8) is to limit the protection based on being obliged to disclose to cases where there is no exception to that obligation and cases where an exception that could have applied to protect the informant (such as public interest immunity) has been raised.

423.   *Subsection (10)* provides that disclosing information in contravention of an investigation anonymity order is a criminal offence. A person who is guilty of this offence is liable to imprisonment and/or a fine. On summary conviction the maximum term of imprisonment is 12 months (or, in Northern Ireland, six months). Following conviction on indictment, the maximum term of imprisonment is five years. However, *subsections (3) to (8)* set out the circumstances in which an order will not be contravened.

424.   *Subsection (13)* defines the term "specified" as meaning specified in the investigation anonymity order.

Section 77: Applications
425.   *Subsection (1)* provides that an application must be made to a justice of the peace. A justice of the peace includes any person acting as such, whether a lay justice, or a judge who is a District Judge (Magistrates' Court) (see section 25 of the Courts Act 2003), or a Crown Court judge (see section 66 of the Courts Act 2003).

426.   The subsection also restricts the availability of investigation anonymity orders to investigating authorities and certain prosecutors. Only certain persons in those organisations (and persons to whom they delegate the function under section 81) may apply for an order. Those persons are described in *subsection (1)(a) to (g)*:

(a) in a case where a police force in England and Wales is conducting the qualifying criminal investigation, the chief officer of police of the police force;

(b) in a case where the British Transport Police Force is conducting the qualifying criminal investigation, the Chief Constable of the British Transport Police Force;

(c) in a case where the Serious Organised Crime Agency is conducting the qualifying criminal investigation, the Director General of the Serious Organised Crime Agency;

(d) in a case where the Police Service of Northern Ireland is conducting the qualifying criminal investigation, the Chief Constable of the Police Service of Northern Ireland;

(e) the Director of Public Prosecutions;

(f) the Director of Revenue and Customs Prosecutions; and

(g) the Director of Public Prosecutions for Northern Ireland.

427.   *Subsection (2)* makes it clear that the applicant is not obliged to give notice of the application to a suspect or someone who has been charged with an offence subject to a qualifying criminal investigation (or their legal representatives). Such notice could defeat the purpose of the order.

428.   *Subsection (3)* requires the applicant to inform the justice of the peace of the identity of the person whose identity is to be protected by the investigation anonymity order. However, the justice of the peace can direct the identity of that person to be withheld.

429.   *Subsection (4)* permits a justice of the peace to grant an application on the papers, without an oral hearing. The Government expects, however, that in the vast majority of cases there will be an oral hearing.

430.   *Subsection (5)* provides that where a justice of the peace determines an application without a hearing the designated officer in relation to that justice of the peace must notify the applicant about the decision, and *subsection (6)* makes similar provision for Northern Ireland.

431.   *Subsection (7)* provides the Secretary of State with a power to amend subsection (1) by order. This will allow the persons who may make an application to be altered. There may for example be amendments because of changes to investigating or prosecuting organisations. The order-making power will also allow for consequential changes for example to section 81 (see *subsection (8)*).

Section 78: Conditions for making order
432.   This section sets out the conditions that have to be satisfied when an application for an investigation anonymity order is made.

433.   Under *subsection (2)*, an investigation anonymity order may be made where the justice of the peace is satisfied that there are reasonable grounds for believing that the five conditions specified in *subsections (3) to (8)* are satisfied. This is to avoid placing an unduly high burden of proof on the applicant, particularly at the early stages of an investigation when the information available may be limited but an investigation anonymity order in respect of a particular informant is highly desirable in order to progress the investigation.

434.   The condition in *subsection (3)* is that a qualifying offence has been committed. (Qualifying offence is defined in section 74.)

435.   The condition in *subsection (4)* is that the person likely to have committed the offence was at least 11 but under 30 years old at the time the offence was committed.

436.   The condition set out in *subsections (5) and (6)*, is that the person likely to have committed the offence is a member of a group (1) which it is possible to identify from the criminal activities that its members appear to be engaged in and (2) it appears that the majority of the members of the group are at least 11 but under 30 years old. The reason for the conditions in subsections (4) to (6) is that the provisions are targeted at informants in qualifying criminal investigations who are afraid of reprisals from street gangs. The age range set out is the understood age range for membership of such gangs, and the activities are the understood activities of such gangs.

437.   The condition in *subsection (7)* is that the informant in respect of whom the order would be made has reasonable grounds to fear intimidation or harm if he or she were identified as a person who is or was able or willing to assist in the investigation into the homicide at issue.

438.   The condition in *subsection (8)* has two limbs, both of which must be satisfied. The first is that the person who would be specified in the order, is able to provide information that would assist the qualifying criminal investigation, and the second is that that person is more likely than not to provide the information if the order was made.

439.   *Subsection (9)* provides that where more than one person is suspected of having caused the death under investigation, the five conditions need be satisfied only in relation to one of the suspects.

440.   *Subsection (10)* gives power to the Secretary of State to modify or repeal subsections (4) to (6) and subsection (9) by order. The conditions set out in subsections (3), (7) and (8) cannot therefore be modified or repealed using this power. This order making power is subject to the affirmative resolution procedure (see section 176(4)(a) and (5)(c)).

441.   *Subsection (11)* provides that an order made under subsection (10) may modify any provision of this Chapter.

Section 79: Appeal against refusal of order
442.   *Subsection (1)* permits an applicant to appeal to a judge of the Crown Court if the justice of the peace refuses the application for an investigation anonymity order.

443.   *Subsection (2)* requires that in order to appeal a refusal of an application, the applicant must indicate an intention to appeal a refusal either in the application for the order or before the justice of the peace at the hearing if there is one. Otherwise no appeal will be possible.

444.   *Subsections (3) and (4)* provide that if the applicant has given an indication of intention to appeal, in the event of a refusal of the application the justice must nevertheless make the investigation anonymity order which has been applied for. The order will continue in force until the appeal is determined or disposed of. This is to err on the side of caution and to protect the informant's identity until such time as the appeal has been dealt with.

445. Subsection (5) provides that where an appeal is made the judge must consider afresh the application for an investigation anonymity order and section 77(3) to (5) applies accordingly to the determination of the application by the judge.

Section 80: Discharge of order
446.   Situations may arise in which an investigation anonymity order should be discharged, for example, where the informant no longer has any fear of reprisals. *Subsection (1)* therefore permits a justice of the peace to discharge an investigation anonymity order if it appears to the justice to be appropriate to do so.

447.   *Subsection (2)* provides that a justice of the peace may discharge an investigation anonymity order on an application by the person who applied for the original order or on an application by the Director of Public Prosecutions, the Director of Revenue and Customs Prosecutions, the Director of Public Prosecutions for Northern Ireland or the informant in respect of whom the order was made.

448.   Under *subsections (3) and (8)* an application for the discharge of an investigation anonymity order may be made only if there has been a material change of circumstances since the order was originally made, or since the last application to discharge the order was made. It will be for the justice of the peace to determine what amounts to a material change in circumstances.

449.   *Subsection (4)* provides that where a person applies for the discharge of an investigation anonymity order any other person who is eligible to apply for the discharge of the order is entitled to be party to the proceedings.

450.   *Subsection (5)* provides that if an application to discharge an investigation anonymity order is made by a person other than the informant in respect of whom the order was made, the justice may not determine the application unless (a) the informant has had an opportunity to oppose the application, or (b) the justice is satisfied that it is not reasonably practicable to communicate with the informant.

451.   *Subsection (6)* provides a party to the proceedings with a right to appeal the justice of the peace's decision to a judge of the Crown Court.

452.   *Subsection (7)* provides that if a party to the proceedings indicates an intention to appeal against a determination to discharge the investigation anonymity order, a justice of the peace who makes such a determination must provide for the discharge of the order not to have effect until the appeal is disposed of.

Section 81: Delegation of functions
453.   By virtue of section 77, the power to apply for an investigation anonymity order is vested in a number of individuals, such as the chief officer of police of a police force. Section 81 makes provision for those individuals to delegate their functions in relation to investigation anonymity orders to other persons. It would not be conducive to operational efficiency for chief officers to deal with every order personally.

Section 82: Public interest immunity
454.   This section provides that this Chapter of the Act does not affect the common law rules on public interest immunity.

Section 83: Review
455.   This section requires the Secretary of State to undertake a review of the operation of investigation anonymity orders and provide Parliament with a report of the review within two years of the commencement of section 77.

Section 84: Application to armed forces
456.   By *subsection (1)*, the provisions of this Chapter of the Act do not apply to investigations concerning service offences as defined by the Armed Forces Act 2006. However, *subsections (2) and (3)* give power to the Secretary of State to make provision by order equivalent to the provisions in this Chapter for that sort of investigation (subject to any modifications the Secretary of State considers appropriate). Provision may be made in such way as the Secretary of State considers appropriate, including applying any of the provisions of this Chapter, with or without modifications. This will allow the Secretary of State to provide for the use of investigation anonymity orders in investigations concerning service offences. An order made under this power is subject to the negative resolution procedure (section 176(4)).

Section 85: Interpretation of this Chapter
457.   Section 85 defines terms which are used in this Chapter of the Act.

Chapter 2: Anonymity of witnesses

Section 86: Witness anonymity orders
458.   *Subsection (1)* sets out what a witness anonymity order is. Breach of the order by the unauthorised disclosure of a witness's identity will fall to be dealt with as contempt of court. Subsection (1) defines the order in such a way as to grant the court a wide discretion as to how the court protects the anonymity of a witness in any particular case. For example, in some cases the court might consider that it is only necessary to screen the witness from the defendant and public; in others it might think it necessary to apply a whole range of measures.

459.   *Subsection (2)* lists the kinds of measures the court may use to secure the witness's anonymity. The list is only illustrative; the court may employ other measures if it thinks fit. Technological developments and the practical arrangements in the court may affect such decisions.

460.   Under *subsection (4)* the court may not make a witness anonymity order which prevents the judge, magistrates or jury either from seeing the witness or from hearing the witness's natural voice. The judge, magistrates and jury must always be able to see and hear the witness.

Section 87: Applications

461.   *Subsection (1)* provides that applications for a witness anonymity order may be made by defendants as well as prosecutors. This reflects the position in the case of *Davis*, where the Court of Appeal allowed a defence witness as well as prosecution witnesses to give evidence anonymously. The Government expects that defence applications are most likely to be made in multi-handed cases (that is, where there is more than one defendant) where one defendant does not wish a witness's identity to be known by the other defendant or defendants. But this subsection does not exclude the possibility of a defence application in a single-handed case.

462.   *Subsection (2)* provides that, where an application for a witness anonymity order is made by the prosecutor, the identity of witnesses may be withheld from the defence before and during the making of the application. This ensures that the operation of the legislation is not impeded by procedural challenges to the power of the prosecution to withhold this information pending the court's determination of the application for the witness anonymity order.

463.   Subsection (2) therefore provides that prosecutors are under no obligation to disclose the witness's identity to the defence at the application stage but must inform the court of the identity of the witness. Similar provision is made for the defence in *subsection (3)*, except that the defence must always disclose the identity of the witness to the prosecutor and the court but do not have to disclose it to any other defendant.

464.   In addition, *subsection (4)* provides that where the prosecution or the defendant proposes to make an application for a witness anonymity order, information that might identify the witness can be taken out of any relevant material which is disclosed before the application has been determined. This does not, however, override the obligation to disclose the identity of the witness to the court (in the case of a prosecution application) or to the court and prosecutor (in the case of a defence application).

465.   Subsection (2) also enables the court to direct that it should not be informed of the identity of the witness. This provides for the possibility that, whilst in the vast majority of cases the court will require to be informed of the witness's identity, there may be rare cases (particularly national security related cases) where even the court will neither need nor wish to know it.

466.   *Subsections (6) and (7)* set out two basic principles. *Subsection (6)* states that on an application for a witness anonymity order every party to the proceedings must be given the opportunity to be heard. However, it may be necessary in the course of making the application to reveal some or all of the very information to which the application relates: for example, the name and address of the witness who is fearful of being identified. So *subsection (7)* provides that the court has the power to hear any party without a defendant or his or her legal representatives being present. This reflects the existing practice, by which prosecution applications are expected to be made in the absence of any other parties in the case, with the defence able to make representations later at a hearing with the prosecution (and possibly other defendants) present. It is expected that defence applications will be permitted without other defendants being present but will always be made in the presence of the prosecution.

467.   *Subsection (8)* confirms that this section does not affect the power of the Criminal Procedure Rule Committee to set out further procedures relating to witness anonymity in the Criminal Procedure Rules.

Section 88: Conditions for making order
468.   *Subsection (2)* requires three conditions to be met before a court can make a witness anonymity order. They are described as conditions A, B and C.

469.   *Subsection (3)* sets out condition A, which is that the measures to be specified in the order are necessary for one of two reasons. The first is to protect the safety of the witness or another person or to prevent serious damage to property. There is no requirement for any actual threat to the witness or any other person. The second is to prevent real harm to the public interest. This will cover the public interest in national security and in the ability of police or other agencies to conduct undercover work.

470.   *Subsection (4)* sets out condition B, which is that the effect of the order would be consistent with the defendant receiving a fair trial. Thus the grant of the order must be compliant with Article 6 of the ECHR.

471.   *Subsection (5)* sets out condition C, which is that the witness's testimony is such that in the interests of justice the witness ought to testify and that either the witness would not testify if the order was not made or there would be real harm to the public interest if the witness were to testify without an order being made (such harm might, for example, arise as a result of the identity of a member of the security services being made public).

472.   *Subsection (6)* specifies that in determining for the purposes of condition A whether the order is necessary to protect the safety of the witness, another person or to prevent damage to property, the court must have regard to the witness's reasonable fear of death or injury either to himself or herself or to another person ("we'll get your kids") or reasonable fear that there would be serious damage to property ("we'll fire-bomb your house").

Section 89: Relevant considerations
473.   *Subsection (1)* requires the court to have regard to the considerations set out in *subsection (2)* when deciding whether to make an order. The court must also have regard to any other factors it considers relevant.

474.   The considerations in subsection (2) are the defendant's general right to know the identity of a witness, the extent to which credibility of the witness is relevant in assessing the weight of the evidence he or she gives, whether the witness's evidence might be the sole or decisive evidence, whether the witness's evidence can be properly tested without knowing the witness's identity, whether the witness has a tendency or any motive to be dishonest and whether alternative means could be used to protect the witness.

Section 90: Warning to jury

475. This section requires the judge to warn the jury in a Crown Court trial, in such way as the judge considers appropriate, so as to ensure that the fact that the order was made does not prejudice the defendant. The provision is based on section 32 of the Youth Justice and Criminal Evidence Act 1999 (the 1999 Act) which makes similar provision for jury warnings where a special measures direction has been made to assist a vulnerable or intimidated witness.

Section 91: Discharge or variation of order

476. The Act does not provide for a right of appeal against the making of, or refusal to make, a witness anonymity order. The Government considers that existing appeal procedures are sufficient. Thus in the case of the prosecutor, the appeal against a terminating ruling under Part 9 of the 2003 Act or Part IV of the Criminal Justice (Northern Ireland) Order 2004 is available. In the case of a defendant, the matter may be raised on appeal against conviction. Section 91 does however provide for the court that made an order to discharge or vary it in those proceedings, either on an application by a party to the proceedings or on its own initiative. This power may be used where, for example, a witness who previously gave evidence anonymously is content for the anonymity to be lifted.

477. Under *subsection (3)* the court must give every party to the proceedings an opportunity to be heard before determining an application for variation or discharge of an order or before varying or discharging an order on its own initiative.

Section 92: Discharge or variation after proceedings

478. This section provides the court that makes a witness anonymity order with the power to discharge or vary that order after the proceedings have finished. The court may vary or discharge the order either on an application by a party to the proceedings or on an application made by the witness. This may be appropriate for example, if a considerable period of time has elapsed since the trial and the circumstances of the witness have changed.

479. *Subsection (4)* requires that the court, prior to discharging or varying a witness anonymity order, provide all parties to the proceedings and the witness the opportunity to be heard unless it is not reasonably practicable to do so, for example, if it is not possible to trace the person concerned.

Section 93: Discharge or variation by appeal court

480. This section provides that an "appeal court" (defined in *subsection (6)* as the Court of Appeal, Court of Appeal in Northern Ireland or Court Martial Appeal Court) can discharge or vary a witness anonymity order made in the proceedings which gave rise to the appeal. Under this Chapter as under the CEWAA, an appeal court already has the power to make a witness anonymity order itself. However, this power does not of itself give it the power to discharge or vary an order made by the lower court.

481. This section gives an appeal court the flexibility it requires. There is no provision for an application procedure: it is intended that the power will be exercised by the appeal court of its own motion, how and when it thinks fit. The provision also applies to witness anonymity orders made under the CEWAA (see paragraph 16 of Schedule 22).

482.   *Subsection (1)* sets out that the power applies where a court has made a witness anonymity order in a criminal trial and the defendant has been convicted, found not guilty by reason of insanity or been found to be under a disability and to have done the act charged. The new power will therefore apply in any appeal against conviction or other finding.

483.   *Subsection (2)* gives an appeal court the discretion to take into account a wide range of factors before discharging or varying an anonymity order.

484.   *Subsection (3)* requires the appeal court to hear any representations made by the parties to the trial proceedings, unless it would be impracticable to communicate with them. This mirrors the duty of the lower court to hear representations from the parties before making, discharging or varying an order during the course of the trial.

485.   Under *subsection (4)* the duty to hear representations does not fetter the appeal court's power to hear a party in the absence of one or more of the defendants and their legal representatives.

Section 94: Special provisions for service courts
486.   This section provides for the application of the witness anonymity provisions in relation to criminal proceedings before the service courts. Matters of law arising in the service courts, with the exception of the Court Martial Appeal Court and its successor under the Armed Forces Act 2006, are dealt with by the judge advocate. There are no juries in the service courts but such courts do have lay members. *Subsection (3)* requires the lay members to be warned as to the effect of the making of an order in the same way as juries are warned.

Section 95: Public interest immunity
487.   This section provides that this chapter of the Act does not affect the common law rules on public interest immunity.

Section 96: Power to make orders under the 2008 Act
488.   This section repeals sections 1 to 9 and 14 of the CEWAA, which provide for making a witness anonymity order under that Act. Paragraphs 16 and 17 of Schedule 22 preserve the effect of a witness anonymity order made under the CEWAA before 1 January 2010 and set out how such orders are to operate.

Section 97: Interpretation of this Chapter
489.   This section defines terms which are used in this Chapter of the Act. *Subsection (2)* ensures that where the court that makes a witness anonymity order is a magistrates' court, it will be open to any magistrates' court in the same local justice area (or the same petty sessions district in Northern Ireland) to discharge or vary the order, not only the court that originally made the order. There might otherwise be difficulties if, for example, a member of the court that made the order were to retire.

Chapter 3: Vulnerable and intimidated witnesses

Section 98: Eligibility for special measures: age of child witnesses
490.   Chapter 1 of Part 2 of the 1999 Act enables a court in criminal proceedings to give a direction that one or more special measures should apply to a witness when giving evidence. A special measures direction can only be made in relation to a witness who is eligible for assistance. The criteria for eligibility are also set out in that Part.

491.   Section 98 amends section 16(1)(a) of the 1999 Act so that all persons aged under 18 will automatically qualify as witnesses eligible for assistance under Part 2 of the 1999 Act. Currently, only witness aged under 17 are automatically eligible for assistance.

Section 99: Eligibility for special measures: offences involving weapons
492.   Section 17(1) of the 1999 Act provides that a witness is eligible for assistance if the court is satisfied that the quality of the witness's evidence would be reduced on the grounds of fear or distress about testifying. Section 17(4) of the 1999 Act gives automatic eligibility for complainants in respect of sexual offences who are witnesses. Automatic eligibility means that the court does not need to be satisfied that the quality of the witness's evidence will be diminished for the purposes of establishing eligibility.

493.   Section 99 extends section 17 and gives automatic eligibility for assistance to witnesses in proceedings related to "relevant offences". The court does not need to be satisfied that the quality of the witness's evidence will be diminished for the purposes of establishing eligibility. However under section 19 of the 1999 Act, the court still has to determine whether any of the available special measures will in fact improve the quality of the witness's evidence and consider whether any such measure or measures might inhibit the evidence being effectively tested. Relevant offences are specified gun and knife crimes which are listed in new Schedule 1A to the 1999 Act (inserted by Schedule 14 to the Act). A witness can inform the court that he or she does not wish to be eligible for assistance.

494.   The list of relevant offences is inserted as a new Schedule 1A to the 1999 Act and the list can be amended by order made by the Secretary of State. The effect of *subsection (3)* is that the order-making power is subject to the affirmative resolution procedure.

Section 100: Special measures directions for child witnesses
495.   Section 100 amends section 21 of the 1999 Act so as to modify the "primary rule" that applies to child witnesses. This rule (before amendment of this section) requires all child witnesses to give evidence in chief by a video recorded statement and any further evidence by live link, unless (except for child witnesses in need of "special protection" in certain sexual and other offence cases) the court is satisfied that to do so will not improve the quality of that child's evidence.

496.   *Subsections (2) and (7)* remove the special category of child witnesses who are "in need of special protection". The effect is to place all child witnesses on the same footing, regardless of the offence to which the proceedings relate.

497.   *Subsections (4) and (5)* modify the primary rule so as to allow a child witness to opt out of giving evidence by a combination of video recorded evidence in chief and live link provided the court is satisfied, after taking into account certain factors, that not giving evidence in that way will not diminish the quality of the child's evidence. If as a result of opting out of the primary rule, the child witness would fall to give his or her evidence in court (and not by way of a live link) a secondary requirement applies. This obliges the child witness to give evidence in court in accordance with the special measure in section 23 of the 1999 Act, that is, from behind a screen that shields the witness from viewing the defendant. The secondary requirement does not apply if the court considers it would not maximise the quality of the child's evidence. The child may also opt out of this secondary requirement, subject to the agreement of the court.

498.   *Subsection (6)* inserts new subsection (4C) into section 21 of the 1999 Act which sets out the factors the court must consider in deciding whether the child witness may opt out of the primary rule and also in deciding whether the child witness may opt out of the secondary requirement to give evidence from behind a screen. These are: the witness's age and maturity, the witness's ability to understand the consequences of giving evidence in court rather than via video-recorded statement, any relationship between the witness and accused, the witness's social, cultural and ethnic background, and the nature and circumstances of the offence being tried, as well as any other factors the court considers relevant.

499.   *Subsection (8)* makes related amendments to section 22 of the 1999 Act, which relates to witnesses who attain the age of 18 after the video recorded statement is made.

Section 101: Special provisions relating to sexual offences
500.   Section 101 inserts new section 22A into the 1999 Act. Section 22A makes special provision for complainants in respect of sexual offences tried in the Crown Court. New section 22A(7) and (9) require the admission of the complainant's video-recorded statement under section 27 of the 1999 Act, unless that requirement would not maximise the quality of the complainant's evidence.

501.   New section 22A(1) and (3) establish that this new section will apply if the complainant of a sexual offence is a witness in proceedings relating to that sexual offence, but not if the witness is under 18 years old (the rules set out in section 21 apply to a witness under 18). Also the requirement to admit the video recorded evidence in chief only applies if a party to the proceedings makes an application requesting that it should be admitted.

502.   New section 22A(2) excludes proceedings in magistrates' courts from these provisions. This does not mean that video recorded evidence in chief is not admissible in such proceedings, but only that the rule in section 22A in favour of admitting such evidence does not apply.

Section 102: Evidence by live link: presence of supporter
503.   Section 24 of the 1999 Act enables the court to make a direction allowing a witness to give evidence by live link. Section 102 amends this section so that the court, when making such a direction can also direct that a person specified by the court can accompany the witness when the witness is giving evidence by live link. The court must take the witness's wishes into account when it determines who is to accompany the witness.

Section 103: Video recorded evidence in chief: supplementary testimony
504.   Section 27 of the 1999 Act enables the court to give a special measures direction that allows a video recorded statement to be admitted as a witness's evidence in chief. Section 103 amends this section so as to relax the restrictions on a witness giving additional evidence in chief after the witness's video-recorded statement has been admitted.

505.   *Subsection (2)* removes the prohibition on asking a witness questions about matters the court considers have been covered adequately in the recorded statement. The effect of this is that the witness may be asked additional questions regarding:

- matters that are not covered in the recorded statement (as is now the case under section 27 of the 1999 Act), and

- matters that are covered in the recorded statement (so long as the permission of the court is given).

506.   *Subsections (3) and (4)* remove the requirement that where an application to ask additional questions is made by a party, the court can give permission to ask a witness supplementary questions only if there has been a material change in circumstances since the court gave the direction to admit the recording.

Section 104: Examination of accused through intermediary
507.   The powers of the court under Chapter 1 of Part 2 of the 1999 Act to make directions allowing for special measures when giving evidence do not apply where the witness is the accused. Chapter 1A gives the court more limited powers regarding the evidence of accused persons. Section 104 increases these powers by adding sections 33BA and 33BB to Chapter 1A. These new sections provide for the use of an intermediary where certain vulnerable accused persons are giving evidence in court.

508.   Subsections (1) and (2) of new section 33BA provide that the court may make a direction allowing an intermediary in any proceedings if the accused satisfies either the condition in subsection (5) or the conditions in subsection (6) and making the direction is necessary to ensure that the accused receives a fair trial.

509.   Subsections (3) and (4) of new section 33BA set out the nature of a direction and the role of the intermediary when the accused gives evidence. The intermediary relays questions that are put to the accused and relays the answers to the questioner. In doing so the intermediary can explain to the accused what the questions mean and to the questioner what the answers mean. Subsection (3) requires the intermediary to be a person approved by the court.

510.   Subsection (5) of new section 33BA sets out the condition that is to be satisfied before a court may allow an accused aged under 18 to use an intermediary. This is that the accused's ability to participate effectively in the trial in terms of giving oral evidence as a witness is compromised by his or her level of intellectual ability or social functioning.

511.   Subsection (6) of new section 33BA sets out the condition applying to an accused who is 18 years or older. The condition is that the accused is prevented from participating effectively as a witness giving oral evidence because the accused has a mental disorder (as defined by the Mental Health Act 1983) or a significant impairment of intelligence and social function.

512.   Subsections (7) and (8) of new section 33BA are about the manner in which an examination through an intermediary is to be conducted, whether or not other provision about the examination is made. The examination is to take place in circumstances which enable the judge or justices, the legal representatives, the jury and a co-accused to see and hear the examination and also enable the judge or justices and the legal representatives to communicate with the intermediary.

513.   Subsections (9) and (10) of new section 33BA require intermediaries to declare that they will perform the role faithfully and extend the Perjury Act 1911 to persons in the role of an intermediary. This is the same obligation that applies to foreign language interpreters and also to intermediaries assisting witnesses under section 29 of the 1999 Act.

514.   New section 33BB gives the court power to discharge a direction for the use of an intermediary where this is no longer necessary for the purposes of a fair trial. The court may also vary a direction. A court must state publicly its reasons for discharging or varying an intermediary direction. This accords with similar provisions in section 20 of the 1999 Act that apply to special measures directions made in respect of witnesses.

Section 105: Age of child complainant
515.   Section 35 of the 1999 Act prevents the cross-examination of a "protected witness" by an accused in person. The definition of a "protected witness" includes a child. Section 105 amends the definition of "child" in section 35 of the 1999 Act to mean a person under the age of 18 (as opposed to 17).

Chapter 4: Live links

Section 106: Directions to attend through live link

516.   *Subsection (2)* amends section 57B of the Crime and Disorder Act 1998, which makes provision for courts to give live link directions for preliminary hearings where the defendant is in custody. The effect of the provision is to enable a single justice of the peace to give or rescind such a direction, thus obviating the need to convene a full court for that purpose.

517.   *Subsection (3)* amends section 57C of the Crime and Disorder Act 1998 by removing the requirement for the defendant's consent to the use of a live link for a preliminary hearing in a magistrates' court where the defendant is at the police station, whether detained there in connection with the offence or having returned to answer live link bail (subsection (3)(b)). It also adds a requirement for the court to be satisfied that a live link direction would not be contrary to the interests of justice (subsection (3)(a)) and removes the ability of a court to rescind a live link direction before the hearing (subsection (3)(c)).

518.   *Subsection (4)* amends section 57D of the Crime and Disorder Act 1998 by removing the requirement for a defendant's consent to be sentenced by live link where he or she has pleaded guilty at a live link preliminary hearing. The subsection adds a requirement for the court to be satisfied that the defendant continuing to attend through the live link would not be contrary to the interests of justice. The separate requirement for the defendant's consent if he or she is to give oral evidence at this kind of live link sentencing hearing is also removed.

519.   *Subsection (5)* amends section 57E of the Crime and Disorder Act 1998 by removing the need for the defendant's consent for a live link sentencing hearing where he or she has previously been convicted of the offence and is in custody. The separate requirement for the defendant's consent if he or she is to give oral evidence at this kind of live link sentencing hearing is also removed.

Section 107: Answering to live link bail

520.   This section amends section 46ZA of the Police and Criminal Evidence Act 1984 (which sets out the circumstances in which a person answering live link bail may be treated as being in police detention), and section 46A(1ZA) of that Act, by making changes that are consequential on the removal of the consent requirement by section 106.

Section 108: Searches of persons answering to live link bail

521.   *Subsection (1)* amends the Police and Criminal Evidence Act 1984 by inserting new sections 54B and 54C giving police the power to search defendants attending the police station for the purposes of answering live link bail. Such searches would at present depend on defendants giving their consent to be searched, as they are not treated as in police detention when they enter a police station in answer to live link bail and the existing powers of search in that Act therefore do not apply to them.

522.   Subsections (2) and (3) of new section 54B provide that a constable may seize and retain anything found on the defendant if the constable reasonably believes it may jeopardise the maintenance of order in the station, endanger anyone in the police station, or be evidence relating to an offence. New section 54B(4) provides that a constable may record any or all of the items seized and retained.

523.   Subsections (5) and (6) of new section 54B provide that the constable searching must be of the same sex as the defendant and that the constable may not carry out an intimate search.

524.   New section 54C(1) provides that anything seized and retained under new section 54B(2) must be returned to the defendant when he or she leaves the police station. However, this is subject to subsections (2) and (3) of new section 54C which provide that items can continue to be retained by a constable:

- in order to establish the lawful owner of the item, where there are reasonable grounds for believing that it has been obtained in consequence of the commission of an offence, or

- if the item is evidence of or relating to an offence, for use as evidence at trial for an offence or for forensic examination or investigation in connection with an offence unless a photograph or copy of the item would be sufficient for that purpose (new section 54C(4)).

525.   New section 54C(5) preserves the power of a court to make an order under section 1 of the Police (Property) Act 1897.

526.   *Subsection (2)* of section 108 inserts new subsection (1ZB) into section 46A of the Police and Criminal Evidence Act 1984 which extends the power of arrest for failure to answer to police bail to include defendants who attend the police station to answer live link bail but refuse to be searched under the new section 54B.

527.   *Subsection (3)* of the section inserts a new paragraph 27A into Part 3 of Schedule 4 to the Police Reform Act 2002, to ensure that designated detention officers, as well as constables, can use the powers in new sections 54B and 54C to search and seize. Where a detention officer exercises the power to seize things found pursuant to a search the officer must deliver the things seized to a constable as soon as practicable and in any case before the person from whom it was seized leaves the police station.

Section 109: Use of live link in certain enforcement hearings
528.   *Subsection (1)* of this section adds a new section 57F to the Crime and Disorder Act 1998 to permit a live link direction to be given in respect of hearings held to enforce a confiscation order, in much the same way as for preliminary hearings under section 57B of that Act. This will enable enforcement proceedings in respect of confiscation orders made against persons who are in custody having been sentenced for the substantive matter to take place by live link between the prison and the magistrates' court.

529.   Subsection (1) of the new section 57F sets out the conditions for making a live link direction in enforcement proceedings for confiscation orders. Subsection (4) of the new section provides that the direction may be given by the court of its own motion or on application by a party to the proceedings. The court may rescind a live link direction at any time before or during the hearing (new section 57F(5)); the court must allow the parties to the proceedings to make representations before giving or rescinding such a direction (new section 57F(6)), and if the person in respect of whom the order has been made is to give oral evidence at this type of hearing, the court must be satisfied that it is not contrary to the interests of justice for him or her to do so (new section 57F(8)). The powers to give and rescind a direction are exercisable by a single justice of the peace (new section 57F(10)).

530.   Subsection (2) makes necessary consequential amendments and defines the types of confiscation order in respect of which a direction under the new section 57F may be given.

Section 110: Direction of registrar for appeal hearing by live link
531.   This section permits the power to give a live link direction for hearings in the Court of Appeal to be exercised by the registrar.

Chapter 5: Miscellaneous

Section 111: Effect of admission of video recording
532.   Section 111 repeals section 138(1) of the 2003 Act. The repealed subsection provides that where an eyewitness's video recorded evidence in chief has been admitted as evidence under section 137 of that Act, the eyewitness cannot give further evidence in chief about a matter which, in the opinion of the court, is adequately covered in the recording.

Section 112: Admissibility of evidence of previous complaints
533.   Section 120 of the 2003 Act provides for the admission of certain previous statements of witnesses and is part of the code on hearsay evidence set out in that Act.

534.   A previous statement will be admissible as evidence of the facts contained within it as if it were oral evidence provided the witness who made it is called to give evidence in the relevant proceedings, states that he or she made the previous statement and believes it to be true, and one of the following also applies:

- section 120(5) – the statement describes or identifies a person, place or thing:

- section 120(6) – the statement was made when matters were fresh in the witness's memory and he or she cannot reasonably be expected to remember the matters stated;

- section 120(7) – the statement consists of a complaint by the victim of the alleged offence which satisfies various requirements including the requirement that it was made as soon as could reasonably be expected after the alleged conduct.

535.   Section 112 amends section 120(7) of the 2003 Act so as to remove the requirement that "the complaint was made as soon as could reasonably be expected after the alleged conduct". Provided the other criteria for admissibility set out in section 120(7) are met, such complaints will be admissible regardless of when they were made.

Section 113: Powers in respect of offenders who assist investigations and prosecutions

536.   The 2005 Act creates a statutory framework to clarify and strengthen common law provisions that provide for immunity and sentence reductions for defendants who co-operate in the investigation and prosecution of others who may have committed criminal offences. Section 71 of that Act confers on a "specified prosecutor" (as defined in section 71(4)) power to grant a person immunity from prosecution. Section 72 of the 2005 Act confers on specified prosecutors power to give an undertaking that any information which a person provides will not be used against that person in any criminal proceedings, or proceedings under Part 5 of the Proceeds of Crime Act 2002 (POCA), which are brought in England and Wales or Northern Ireland. Section 73 of the 2005 Act gives specified prosecutors power to enter into a written agreement with a defendant, for the defendant to provide assistance in relation to an offence and provides for the court to take into account the assistance given or offered when determining the sentence to impose on the defendant. There is also a power in section 74 for specified prosecutors to refer a case back to the court where a defendant benefits from a sentence reduction but then reneges on the agreement to provide assistance.

537.   *Subsections (2) and (5)* of section 113 amend section 71(1) and section 72(1) of the 2005 Act to provide that these provisions can only be used for the investigation or prosecution of serious criminal offences. While a person who assists the authorities under these powers can be offered immunity or a restricted use undertaking or sentence reduction agreement for *any* offence, the assistance must be in relation to the investigation or prosecution of an offence that is capable of being tried in the Crown Court (that is it is either an indictable offence or triable either way).

538.   *Subsection (3)* amends section 71 of the 2005 Act by adding the FSA and the Secretary of State for BIS to the list of "specified prosecutors" who can use the powers set out in sections 71 to 74 of the 2005 Act.

539.   *Subsection (4)* adds new subsections (6A) to (6C) to section 71 of the 2005 Act. New subsection (6C) provides that the power of the FSA and BIS to grant immunity from prosecution under section 71 in any case is subject to the consent of the Attorney General. This reflects the fact that the other "specified prosecutors" under the 2005 Act are superintended by the Attorney General and the Attorney General is consulted before any grant of immunity is made by a superintended prosecutor. The requirement that the FSA and BIS obtain the Attorney General's consent before granting immunity under section 71 is aimed at putting FSA and BIS in a comparable position to the other "specified prosecutors" when granting immunity under section 71 of the 2005 Act.

540.   New subsection (6A) provides that the FSA and BIS may delegate the powers in sections 71 to 74 of the 2005 Act within their respective organisations only to one prosecutor (or a nominated deputy in that person's absence). New subsection (6B) disapplies the normal arrangements for discharging the functions of the FSA in order to ensure that these powers are delegated only in the circumstances set out in new subsection (6A).

541.   *Subsection (7)* introduces a new section 75B which provides the Attorney General with the power to issue guidance to all the "specified prosecutors" on the use of the powers set out at sections 71 to 74 of the 2005 Act.

Section 114: Bail: assessment of risk of committing an offence causing injury
542.   Section 114 amends Schedule 1 to the Bail Act 1976.

543.   *Subsection (2)* provides that a defendant who is charged with murder may not be granted bail unless the court is of the opinion that there is no significant risk that, if released on bail, he or she would commit an offence that would be likely to cause physical or mental injury to another person.

544.   *Subsection (3)(a)* provides that, in deciding whether it is of the opinion that there is no such significant risk, the court must have regard to any relevant considerations in paragraph 9 of Part 1 of Schedule 1 to the Bail Act 1976.

545.   *Subsection (3)(b)* amends paragraph 9 in relation to bail decisions where the alleged offence is imprisonable and triable in the Crown Court. It provides that, in deciding whether to grant bail in a case where the court is satisfied that there are substantial grounds for believing the person would commit an offence while on bail, the court must have regard to the risk that such further offending would, or would be likely to, cause physical or mental injury to another person.

Section 115: Bail decisions in murder cases to be made by a Crown Court judge
546.   Section 115 provides that a person who is charged with murder (including one charged with murder and other offences – *subsection (6)*) may not be granted bail except by a judge of the Crown Court. The power of magistrates to consider bail in murder cases, whether at the first hearing or after a breach of an existing bail condition, is thus removed.

547.   *Subsection (3)* provides that where a person charged with murder appears, or is brought before, a magistrates' court, a bail decision must be made by a judge of the Crown Court as soon as reasonably practicable, and in any event within 48 hours (excluding public holidays – *subsection (7)*) beginning with the day after the person's appearance in the magistrates' court.

548.   *Subsection (4)* provides that the person must if necessary be committed in custody to the Crown Court to enable a bail decision to be made, and *subsection (5)* that it is immaterial whether he or she is at the same time sent for trial or remanded following adjournment of proceedings under section 52 of the Crime and Disorder Act 1998. That section generally requires a defendant charged with an offence only triable in the Crown Court to be sent by the magistrates' court to the Crown Court forthwith.

Section 116: Indictment of offenders
549.   The need for section 116 arises from the decision of the House of Lords in *R v Clarke, R v McDaid* [2008] UKHL 8. Under section 2 of the Administration of Justice (Miscellaneous Provisions) Act 1933 (the 1933 Act), a bill of indictment becomes an indictment upon which a trial on indictment may proceed only once the bill has been signed by a proper officer of the court. Where a trial proceeds without a bill of indictment having been signed, the House of Lords confirmed in these cases that those proceedings and any subsequent conviction and sentence will be invalid as signature of the bill of indictment is a necessary prerequisite to the Crown Court obtaining jurisdiction to try the case.

550.   Section 116 removes from section 2 of the 1933 Act the requirement that a bill of indictment be signed by the proper officer of the court with the result that the bill becomes an indictment on being preferred (*subsection (1)(a) and (b)*). Subsection (1)(c) inserts into section 2 of the 1933 Act three new subsections which provide that objections to an indictment based on an alleged failure to observe procedural rules may not be taken after the start of the trial proper, that is, when the jury has been sworn. (For this purpose a preparatory hearing does not mark the start of trial.)

551.   Subsection (1)(d) and (2) make consequential amendments.

552.   Paragraph 26 of Schedule 22 provides that, for the purposes of any proceedings before a court after the Act is passed, the amendments are deemed always to have had effect. They apply even if the proceedings (including appeals) have begun before the Act was passed.

Section 117: Detention of persons under section 41 of the Terrorism Act 2000
553.   Section 117 provides powers for further scrutiny of the treatment of terrorist suspects detained under section 41 of the Terrorism Act 2000.

554.   *Subsections (1) to (3)* amend section 36 of the Terrorism Act 2006 (review of terrorism legislation) to clarify that the independent reviewer of terrorism legislation may review and report on the treatment of persons detained under section 41 of the Terrorism Act 2000 for more than 48 hours.

555.   *Subections (4) to (8)* amend section 51 of the Police Reform Act 2002 (independent custody visitors for places of detention).

556.   Subsection (5) provides that all police authorities must, in the arrangements they make regarding visits to detainees by independent custody visitors, require independent custody visitors who visit a person detained under section 41 of the Terrorism Act 2000 ("a suspected terrorist detainee") to prepare and submit a report on that visit; and the arrangements must also ensure that a copy of that report is sent to the independent reviewer of terrorism legislation.

557.   Subsection (6) gives independent custody visitors the authority to listen to or view any audio or video recordings made of police interviews with a suspected terrorist detainee. Subsection (7) provides the police with the power to refuse, in certain circumstances, an independent custody visitor access to such recordings, whether in part or whole.

Part 4 - Sentencing

Chapter 1: Sentencing Council for England and Wales

Section 118 and Schedule 15: Sentencing Council for England and Wales
558.   This section establishes the Sentencing Council for England and Wales and introduces Schedule 15 which sets out details of the Council's organisation and membership. Section 135 abolishes the SAP and the SGC.

559.   Schedule 15 sets out the constitution of the Council, and makes provision about the appointment of the chair, deputy chair and members, the terms of appointment of members and the remuneration of members.

560.   The Sentencing Council will consist of 14 members, of whom eight are judicial members and six are non-judicial members.

561.   The judicial members will be appointed by the Lord Chief Justice with the agreement of the Lord Chancellor.

562.   The non-judicial members will be appointed by the Lord Chancellor with the agreement of the Lord Chief Justice.

563.   The Lord Chief Justice will appoint, with the agreement of the Lord Chancellor, one of the judicial members to chair the Council and one judicial member to chair the Council in the absence of the chairing member.

564.   A person is eligible to be appointed as a judicial member if the person is a judge of the Court of Appeal, a puisne judge of the High Court, a circuit judge, a District Judge (Magistrates' Courts) or a lay justice. The eight judicial members must include at least one Circuit judge, one District Judge (Magistrates' Courts) and one lay justice.

565.   The Lord Chancellor will appoint as non-judicial members individuals with experience in one or more of the following areas: criminal defence, criminal prosecution, policing, sentencing policy and the administration of justice, the promotion of the welfare of victims of crime, academic study or research in criminal law or criminology, statistics and the rehabilitation of offenders.

566.   The Lord Chief Justice is to have the title of President of the Sentencing Council of England and Wales although the President is not a member of the Council.

567.   The Lord Chancellor can nominate a representative with experience of sentencing policy to attend and speak at Council meetings.

568.   The Lord Chancellor can make an order with the agreement of the Lord Chief Justice to cover terms of office, re-appointment and removal of members.

569.   The Council's actions will remain valid even if there is a vacancy on the Council or there was a defect in the appointments procedure.

570.   The Lord Chancellor may pay appropriate remuneration and expenses.

Section 119: Annual Report
571.   At the end of each financial year the Council will report on the exercise of its functions to the Lord Chancellor who will lay that report before Parliament.

Section 120: Sentencing guidelines
572.   The Sentencing Council is given the power to prepare sentencing guidelines. Guidelines may be general in nature or specific to an offence or category of offence. The Council must prepare guidelines on the reduction of sentence for a guilty plea, and on the application of the totality principle. The Council may prepare sentencing guidelines about any other sentencing matter.

573.   When it draws up guidelines, the Council must have regard to current sentencing practice, the need to promote consistency in sentencing, the impact of sentencing decisions on victims of crime, the need to promote public confidence in the criminal justice system, the cost of different sentences and their effectiveness in reducing re-offending, and the Council's monitoring of the application of its guidelines.

574.   Guidelines must be published first in draft. The Council must consult on the draft with the Lord Chancellor, with the Justice Select Committee of the House of Commons, with anyone whom the Lord Chancellor directs the Council to consult and with anyone else the Council considers appropriate. After this consultation, the Council may amend its draft and issue definitive guidelines.

575.   The Council has the power to review and revise its guidelines as it considers necessary. If it does so, it must undertake the same consultation process.

Section 121: Sentencing ranges
576.   In the case of offence specific guidelines, the Council is to have regard to the desirability of setting out the guidelines in the way described in section 121. The guidelines should, if reasonably practicable, divide the offence into levels of seriousness based on the offender's culpability and/or the harm caused and any other particularly relevant factors. The guidelines should state the range of sentences appropriate for a court to impose for the offence. If the guidelines divide the offence into levels of seriousness, they should also state the range of sentences appropriate for a court to impose for offences at each level. The guidelines should also specify a starting point in the range or, if the guidelines divide the offence into levels of seriousness, a starting point for each level in the range. The starting point is the sentence the Council considers to be appropriate in a case where the offender has pleaded not guilty and before aggravating or mitigating factors are taken into account.

577.   The guidelines should list any relevant aggravating and mitigating factors that are likely to apply to the offence and the relevant mitigating factors personal to an offender. The guidelines should also include criteria and guidance on the weight to be given to an offender's previous convictions and other aggravating and mitigating circumstances where these are significant to the offence or the offender being sentenced.

578.   The requirement to list mitigating circumstances personal to the offender does not apply to the requirements to take into account in sentencing an early guilty plea or the reduction in sentence for providing assistance (Queen's evidence) or any rule of law as to reducing sentences under the totality principle. Section 120(3) already requires the Council to produce sentencing guidelines dealing with the first and last of these matters.

579.   The provision made in accordance with this section may differ for different circumstances or cases involving the offence.

Section 122: Allocation guidelines
580.   The Council may prepare guidelines for magistrates' courts on how to allocate cases either to a magistrates' court for summary trial or the Crown Court for trial on indictment. In framing or revising allocation guidelines the Council must have regard to the need to promote consistency in allocation decisions and the results of the Council's monitoring.

Section 123: Preparation or revision of guidelines in urgent cases
581.   In a case of urgency, the Council will not be required to go through the normal procedures set out for issuing guidelines if it is impractical to do so. However, the Council must always consult with the Lord Chancellor before issuing definitive guidelines. If the Council does adopt this abbreviated process the Council must state that it is doing so and give its reasons.

Section 124: Proposals by Lord Chancellor or Court of Appeal
582.   The Lord Chancellor can propose to the Council that it prepare or revise its guidelines. If the Court of Appeal is considering an appeal against sentence or an Attorney General's reference case, it may propose to the Council that it prepare or revise sentencing guidelines for an offence relevant to the case it is considering.

583.   The Council must consider a proposal from either the Lord Chancellor or the Court of Appeal.

Section 125: Sentencing Guidelines: duty of court

584.   Every court must, in sentencing an offender, follow any relevant guidelines, unless it is satisfied that it would be contrary to the interests of justice to do so. The interests of justice exception qualifies all the duties mentioned below.   Where there are offence-specific guidelines relevant to the offender's case which are structured in the way set out in section 121(2) to (5) a court must sentence within the offence range set out in the guideline. Where those guidelines specify different levels of seriousness of the offence, the court must if possible decide which category most resembles the offender's case in order to identify the sentencing starting point. The court's duty is to sentence within the range of sentences for the offence as a whole (as opposed to the range specified for the particular level).

585.   The duty to follow sentencing guidelines is subject to various statutory provisions, for example, those which place restrictions on imposing community sentences and imposing discretionary custodial sentences; the requirement that custodial sentences should be for the shortest term commensurate with the seriousness of an offence and the requirements for minimum sentences in certain cases. The duty to impose a sentence within the identified range is subject to the requirements to take into account an early guilty plea, the reduction in sentence for providing assistance (Queen's evidence) and any rule of law as to reducing sentences under the totality principle.

Section 126: Determination of tariffs etc

586.   This section applies where a court is imposing an indeterminate sentence such as a mandatory life sentence, discretionary life sentence, imprisonment for public protection sentence or an extended sentence for certain violent and sexual offences. In these cases, the court is required to follow the guidelines specifying a sentence range when determining the notional determinate term for the purpose of setting a tariff for the indeterminate sentence.

Section 127: Resource implications of guidelines

587.   When the Council issues draft or definitive guidelines it must publish an accompanying resource assessment of the impact of the implementation of the guidelines, setting out the impact on the resources required for the provision of prison places, probation and youth justice services.

588.   In the case of guidelines issued in the case of urgency, the resource assessment should be published as soon as possible after the guidelines have been issued.

589.   The Council must keep its resource assessments under review, and revise them if they become materially inaccurate.

Section 128: Monitoring

590. The Council must monitor the operation and effect of its sentencing guidelines, and consider the conclusions which can be drawn from the information obtained by its monitoring. The Council must, in particular, discharge this duty with a view to drawing conclusions about the frequency with which, and extent to which, sentencers depart from guidelines, the factors which influence sentences imposed by courts, the effect of guidelines on consistency in sentencing and the effect of guidelines on the promotion of public confidence in the criminal justice system. The Council's annual report must include a summary of its monitoring information and a report of any conclusions it has drawn.

Section 129: Promoting awareness

591. The Council must publish, in relation to each local justice area, information on sentencing practice of the magistrates' courts in that area and, in relation to each location at which the Crown Court sits, information on the sentencing practice of the Crown Court sitting in that location.

592. The Council may promote awareness of matters relating to sentencing in England and Wales, including the manner of sentencing, its cost effectiveness and the operation and effect of the guidelines. In particular, it can promote this awareness by publishing data on sentencing.

Section 130: Resources: effect of sentencing practice

593. The Council's annual report must include a sentencing factors report. This report is an assessment by the Council of the effect which any changes to sentencing practice are having or are likely to have on the resources required for the provision of prisons places, probation and youth justice services.

Section 131: Resources: effect of factors not related to sentencing

594. The Council's annual report must discuss any non-sentencing factors which are having, or are likely to have, a significant effect on the resources needed or available for giving effect to the sentences imposed by courts. These factors include recalls to prison, breaches of court orders, patterns of re-offending, actions by the Parole Board, early release and levels of remands in custody. The Council may also report to the Lord Chancellor at any time on the impact of such factors.

Section 132: Duty to assess impact of policy and legislative proposals

595. The Lord Chancellor may refer to the Council any government policy proposal or proposal for legislation which the Lord Chancellor considers may have a significant effect on the resources required for the provision of prison places, probation and youth justice services. The Council must assess any likely effect of the policy or legislation and publish its assessment.

596. For this purpose a government policy proposal or proposal for legislation includes a proposal of the Welsh Ministers, and proposals for primary or subordinate legislation are relevant if, or to the extent that, the legislation extends to England and Wales.

Section 133: Assistance by Lord Chancellor
597.   The Lord Chancellor may, if the Council request it, provide the Council with assistance in carrying out any of its functions, for example, by sharing data or other information with the Council.

Section 134: Entrenchment of Lord Chancellor's functions
598.   This section amends Schedule 7 to the Constitutional Reform Act 2005 so as to provide that all of the functions of the Lord Chancellor in relation to the Council are protected functions of the office.   Protected functions can only be transferred to another Minister by Act of Parliament.

Section 135: Abolition of existing sentencing bodies
599.   This section abolishes the Sentencing Advisory Panel and the Sentencing Guidelines Council.

Section 136: Interpretation of this Chapter
600.   This section sets out the definitions of terms used in this Chapter.

Chapter 2: Other provisions relating to sentencing

Section 137 and Schedule 16: Extension of driving disqualification
601.   Section 137 introduces Schedule 16. *Paragraph 2(2)* of Schedule 16 inserts a new section, section 35A, into the Road Traffic Offenders Act 1988. Section 35A provides for an extension in the length of the period of a driving disqualification imposed under sections 34 and 35 of that Act where a custodial sentence is also imposed for the same offence. The court must determine the appropriate discretionary period of disqualification and then add on the appropriate extension period. This section applies where the offender is convicted in England and Wales.

602.   New section 35A(4) defines the appropriate extension period, which takes account of that part of the sentence which the offender will serve in prison. Where a life sentence or an indeterminate sentence for public protection sentence is imposed the extension period is the period of the minimum tariff set by the court. Where an extended sentence is imposed the extension period is half the custodial term, that is, the period of the sentence to be served in prison. Where a detention and training order is imposed, the extension period is half the term of the order. Once the provisions in section 181 of the 2003 Act are commenced, if custody plus is imposed the extension period is the custodial period specified by the court and if intermittent custody is imposed the extension period is equal to the number of custodial days specified by the court. In all other cases, the extension period is equal to one half of the custodial sentence (at which point the offender is subject to automatic release or, for sentences of 12 months or more, released on licence in the community until the end of sentence).

603.   New section 35A(6) ensures that the appropriate extension period is reduced to reflect any reduction in the custodial sentence as a result of the court taking into account time already served on remand, or periods of remand on bail in a case where the offender was subject to a curfew condition which was electronically monitored.

604.   Under new section 35A(7) the extension of disqualification does not apply where the court imposes a suspended sentence or where a life sentence to which no early release provisions apply (cases where the offender must spend the rest of his or her life in prison).

605.   New sections 35A(8) and (9) provide for an order-making power to amend the extension period where an amending order is made under section 267 of the 2003 Act to change the proportion of time to be served in custody in relation to a standard determinate sentence, or the appropriate custodial term of an extended sentence.

606.   New section 35B deals with offenders who are disqualified at the same time as they are imprisoned for another offence or at a time when they are already in prison for another offence. In respect of these offenders, the court is required to have regard to the diminished effect of disqualification as a distinct punishment where the person who is disqualified is also imprisoned. It is to have regard to that consideration if, and to the extent that, it is appropriate to do so. For example, the more that the beginning of a driving disqualification overlaps with the end of the period of detention under an earlier sentence, the more a court might extend the disqualification to compensate for the diminished effect during the overlap.

607.   *Paragraph 2(3)* of Schedule 16 inserts a new section 35C and section 35D into the Road Traffic Offenders Act 1988, which makes provision equivalent to that made by paragraph 2(2) for cases where the person is convicted in Scotland.

608.   *Paragraph 3* inserts a new sections 248D and 248E into the Criminal Procedure (Scotland) Act 1995 to the same effect as paragraph 2(3) but this time in relation to a person disqualified under section 248 (driving disqualification where vehicle used to commit an offence) or section 248A (general power to disqualify offenders) of that Act. Section 248D applies where the driving disqualification and the sentence of imprisonment are both imposed for the same offence. Section 248E applies where there is an overlap between the period of disqualification and of imprisonment but the overlapping punishments are not imposed for the same offence.

609.   *Paragraphs 1, 4 and 6* of Schedule 16 insert new provisions in the Criminal Justice (Northern Ireland) Order 1980, the Road Traffic Offenders (Northern Ireland) Order 1996 and the Criminal Justice (Northern Ireland) Order 2008 to the same effect as paragraph 2(2) where the person is convicted in Northern Ireland.

610.   *Paragraph 5* of Schedule 16 inserts new sections 147A and 147B into the Powers of Criminal Courts (Sentencing) Act 2000 (the 2000 Act). These sections make similar provision to the new sections inserted by paragraph 2(2), but this time for an extension of the period of the driving disqualification imposed by courts in England and Wales under section 146 (driving disqualification for any offence) or 147 (driving disqualification where vehicle used for the purposes of crime) of that Act. Section 147A applies where a custodial sentence is also imposed for the offence. Section 147B applies where there is an overlap between the period of disqualification and the period of imprisonment but the overlapping punishments are not imposed for the same offence.

Section 138: Dangerous offenders: terrorism offences (England and Wales)
611.   Schedule 15 to the 2003 Act lists specified violent or sexual offences which may attract a sentence of imprisonment for public protection under section 225 of the 2003 Act or an extended sentence under section 227 of the 2003 Act. Section 138 amends Part 1 to Schedule 15 of the 2003 Act (specified violent offences) by inserting certain terrorist offences. All the offences inserted carry a maximum penalty of ten years or more. The changes take effect as provided in section 182 (commencement two months after Act is passed) and paragraph 29 to 36 of Schedule 22 (transitional, transitory and saving provisions).

Section 139: Dangerous offenders: terrorism offences (Northern Ireland)
612.   This section makes amendments to Schedules 1 and 2 to the Criminal Justice (Northern Ireland) Order 2008 to similar effect.

Section 140: Appeals against certain confiscation orders (England and Wales)
613.   Section 140 inserts new subsections into section 11 of the Criminal Appeal Act 1968 ("the 1968 Act") and a new section 11A in relation to defence appeals against the making of confiscation orders. If the Court of Appeal allows an appeal and quashes a confiscation order, the new subsections enable the Court to direct the Crown Court to consider whether a new order should be made, and if so what the order should be, instead of the Court of Appeal having to consider the matter itself.

614.   The effect of section 140 is to give the Court of Appeal the power to remit cases to the Crown Court where a confiscation order made under certain enactments is quashed as a result of a successful appeal by the defence; the relevant enactments are listed in new subsection (3D) inserted into section 11 of the 1968 Act. The Crown Court must comply with any directions given by the Court of Appeal (subsection (3B)) and must ensure that any new order is not more severe than the one that it replaces (subsection (3C)). Section 140 also inserts new section 11A into the 1968 Act, which enables the Crown Court to set sums already confiscated (and paid over) under the terms of the original order against any sums required to be paid under any replacement order.

Section 141: Appeals against certain confiscation orders (Northern Ireland)
615.   Section 141 inserts new subsections into section 10 of the Criminal Appeal (Northern Ireland) Act 1980 and a new section 10A to the Act.

616.   The effect of section 141 on section 10 of the Criminal Appeal (Northern Ireland) Act 1980 is similar to the effect of section 140 on section 11 of the 1968 Act. However, there is no provision stating that the Northern Ireland Court of Appeal must ensure that any new order is not more severe than the one that it replaces. This is because the existing Northern Ireland provision in section 10(3) allows the Court of Appeal to pass more or less severe sentences on appeal.

Part 5 - Miscellaneous criminal justice provisions

Section 142: Commissioner for Victims and Witnesses

617.   A Commissioner for Victims and Witnesses was legislated for in the Domestic Violence, Crime and Victims Act 2004 (sections 48 to 53 and Schedules 8 and 9), but a Commissioner was never appointed and the legislation has not yet been commenced. This section amends sections 48 to 55 of that Act so as to modify the status and functions of the Commissioner. *Subsections (2) and (6)* repeal the provisions in section 48 of, and Schedule 8 to, that Act that establish the Commissioner as a corporation sole, and make new provision in respect of funding.

618.   The core functions of the Commissioner are set out in section 49(1) of the Domestic Violence, Crime and Victims Act 2004. These functions are that the Commissioner must promote the interests of victims and witnesses; take such steps as he or she considers appropriate with a view to encouraging good practice in the treatment of victims and witnesses; and keep under review the operation of the code of practice issued under section 32 of the Domestic Violence, Crime and Victims Act 2004. These core functions remain unchanged.

619.   In addition, under section 49(2) of that Act, the Commissioner, for any purpose connected with the performance of his or her duties, may (a) make proposals to the Secretary of State for amending the code (at the request of the Secretary of State or on his or her own initiative); (b) make a report to the Secretary of State; (c) make recommendations to an authority within his or her remit; (d) undertake or arrange for or support (financially or otherwise) the carrying out of research; and (e) consult any person he thinks appropriate. *Subsection (3)(a)* repeals section 49(2)(d). In future, any such research would be arranged and funded by the Department.

620.   In addition to reports made under section 49(2)(b), new subsections (4) to (7) of section 49 of the Domestic Violence, Crime and Victims Act 2004 require the Commissioner to prepare an annual report. Copies of all reports are to be sent to the Justice Secretary, the Attorney General and the Home Secretary. The Commissioner is responsible for publishing all reports.

621.   *Subsection (4)* amends section 50 of the Domestic Violence, Crime and Victims Act 2004 which sets out when the Commissioner can be required to give advice and to whom. Section 50(2) is repealed so the Commissioner is not required to give advice on the request of "an authority within his or her remit". The Government envisages that such requests can be made through a Minister of the Crown under section 50(1).

622.   Section 55 of the Domestic Violence, Crime and Victims Act 2004 created a Victims Advisory Panel which was set up in October 2006. The terms of reference for the Panel are to advise the Home Secretary, the Lord Chancellor and the Attorney General of the views of victims of crime with particular reference to their interaction with the Criminal Justice System and its agencies. The Panel's remit also includes offering views and advice on the prevention of crime from a victim's perspective and generally contributing to developing and safeguarding the rights of victims. *Subsection (5)* inserts new sections (1A) and (1B) into section 55 which provide for the Commissioner to be a member of the Victims Advisory Panel and to chair the Panel.

Section 143: Implementation of E-Commerce and Services directives: penalties
623.   The section will allow the Government to implement fully Article 30(2) of the Services Directive and Article 3(1) of the E-Commerce Directive.

624.   In both cases the UK is required to extend the powers of its regulatory agencies (competent authorities) so that they are able, if so required, to take action in relation to offences committed by UK-based service providers in other European Union member States.

625.   Both Articles will be implemented by secondary legislation through the powers in section 2(2) of the European Communities Act 1972. However there are limitations in paragraph 1(1)(d) of Schedule 2 to that Act on the penalties that can be imposed by secondary legislation under section 2(2). This section disapplies these limitations for the purposes of the implementation of the Services and E-Commerce Directives. This is so that penalties can be imposed in relation to offences committed by UK-based service providers, whether in the UK or elsewhere in the European Union. Regulations made using this power will be subject to the affirmative resolution procedure.

Section 144 and Schedule 17: Treatment of convictions in other member States etc
626.   Section 144 introduces Schedule 17. Section 144 and Schedule 17 implement the Council of the European Union Framework Decision 2008/675/JHA to ensure that previous convictions in other European Union member States are taken into account in criminal proceedings in England, Wales and Northern Ireland, to the extent that previous United Kingdom convictions are taken into account in criminal proceedings. The Schedule also makes a number of associated changes.

Admission of evidence as to bad character of a defendant
627.   Section 103 of the 2003 Act (which extends to England and Wales only) concerns evidence of a defendant's bad character that is admissible because it is relevant to an important matter in issue between the defendant and the prosecution. Evidence which demonstrates that a defendant has a propensity to commit offences of the kind with which he is charged can be admitted under section 103(1)(a). This includes evidence of previous convictions.

628.   *Paragraph 1(2)* of Schedule 17 amends section 103 of the 2003 Act, by inserting new subsections (7), (8) and (9), so that previous convictions of an offence, under the law of any country outside England and Wales can be admitted as evidence to the same extent as previous convictions in England and Wales, provided that the offence would also be an offence in England and Wales if it were done there at the time of the trial for the offence with which the defendant is now charged. As well as giving effect to the Council Framework Decision (2008/675/JHA) to make it clear that offences committed anywhere in the European Union can be admitted in these circumstances, this amendment puts beyond doubt that previous convictions in any other country can be admitted to the same extent as previous convictions of offences committed in England and Wales.

629.   Section 108 of the 2003 Act (which extends to England and Wales only) deals with the admissibility of certain juvenile convictions. It provides that certain of those convictions (those relating to offences committed under the age of 14 in any trial for an offence committed over the age of 21) fall under the general scheme for admitting evidence in this Part of the Act, and can only be admitted if, firstly, the offence for which the defendant is being tried and the offence for which the defendant was previously convicted are triable only on indictment, and, secondly, the court is satisfied that the interests of justice require the admission of the evidence.

630.   *Paragraph 1(3)* of Schedule 17 amends section 108 by inserting new subsections (2A) and (2B) which extend this section to convictions of offences under the law of a country outside England and Wales, provided that the offence would also have been an offence in England and Wales if it were done there at the time of the proceedings for the offence with which the defendant is now charged. Again, this amendment is to give effect to the Council Framework Decision (2008/675/JHA) to make it clear that offences committed anywhere in the European Union can be admitted, and also to put beyond doubt that previous convictions in other countries can be admitted to the same extent as previous convictions of offences committed in England and Wales.

631.   *Paragraph 2* amends the Criminal Justice (Evidence) (Northern Ireland) Order 2004 (which makes equivalent provision to sections 103 and 108 of the 2003 Act in respect of Northern Ireland) to the same effect in respect of convictions of offences under the law of a country outside Northern Ireland.

Bail
632.   *Paragraph 3* amends section 25 of the Criminal Justice and Public Order Act 1994 (which extends to England and Wales only), which provides that a person charged with homicide or rape who has a previous conviction obtained in the United Kingdom of any such offence or of culpable homicide shall only be granted bail if there are exceptional circumstances which justify it.

633.   The application of section 25 is amended. New subsection (3A) amends the current wording of section 25 to make it clear that the section applies to a person convicted in any part of the UK of an offence specified in subsection (2) (which includes homicide, rape and other sexual offences) or of culpable homicide, and, if that previous conviction was one of manslaughter or culpable homicide, only if that person was then a child or young person and was sentenced to long-term detention under the enactments specified as relevant, or if the person was not then a child or young person, they were sentenced to imprisonment or detention. Under the relevant enactments, only those aged over 21 years of age can be sentenced to imprisonment. Those aged under 21 years can only be sentenced to detention. A child or young person is a person under the age of 18 years.

634.   New subsection (3B) provides that a previous conviction of an offence in another European Union member State which corresponds to a UK offence which would trigger the application of section 25 will cause section 25 to apply. An offence corresponds to a UK offence if it would have constituted that offence if it had been done in the United Kingdom at the time when the offence was committed in the EU member State. As the relevant enactments cannot apply to European Union offences as they only concern domestic situations, the new subsection (3B) uses the term "detention" to cover both what is known in the United Kingdom as "imprisonment" (for offenders aged 21 years and over) and "detention" (for offenders aged under 21), and spells out what amounts to long-term detention under those enactments (detention in excess of two years).

Decision as to allocation
635.   *Paragraphs 4 and 5* amend section 19 of the Magistrates' Courts Act 1980 and paragraph 9 of Schedule 3 to the Crime and Disorder Act 1998 respectively, as substituted by Schedule 3 to the 2003 Act (not yet in force). The existing legislation sets out the criteria for determining whether an offence triable either way should be tried summarily or on indictment by, in the case of the Magistrates' Courts Act 1980 a magistrates' court, or, in the case of the Crime and Disorder Act 1998, a Crown Court. It permits the prosecution to inform the courts of any previous convictions of the defendant, previous convictions being convictions by a court in the United Kingdom or convictions or findings of guilt under service law.

636.   The amendments add to what is a previous conviction to include convictions by a court in another member State, provided that the offence of which the defendant was convicted would also have been an offence in the United Kingdom if it had been done there at the time the allocation decision is made.

Seriousness
637.   *Paragraph 6* of Schedule 17 amends section 143 of the 2003 Act, which sets out the principles the court must follow when determining the seriousness of an offence, in the context of sentencing an offender. Any previous convictions, where they are recent and relevant, must be regarded as an aggravating factor which should increase the severity of the sentence.

638.   Paragraph 6 extends what is a previous conviction to include previous convictions by a court in another European Union member State, provided that the offence would have been an offence in the United Kingdom if it had been done there at the time of the trial of the defendant for the current offence. Paragraph 6 also makes clear that the court is not prevented from treating a previous conviction by a court outside the UK and a European Union member State, or a conviction by a court in a European Union member State of an offence which would not amount to an offence in the UK, as aggravating factors where the court considers it appropriate to do so.

639.   *Paragraph 7* amends section 238 of the Armed Forces Act 2006, which makes equivalent provision to section 143 of the 2003 Act in respect of service offences. Section 238 has been amended in a similar fashion to section 143.

640.   Section 151 of the 2003 Act provides the court with a discretionary power for dealing with persistent petty offenders. Where an offender is aged 16 or over when he is convicted and has been sentenced to a fine on at least three previous occasions, the court may impose a community sentence even if the current offence is one which would on its own warrant a fine only. Section 151 has been amended by the Criminal Justice and Immigration Act 2008 (the 2008 Act), and although these amendments have not yet come into force, the amendments made by paragraph 8 are to section 151 as amended.

641.   *Paragraph 8* of Schedule 17 extends section 151 to require previous convictions by a court in another European Union member State to be taken into account to the same extent as previous convictions in the United Kingdom, provided that the offence to which the conviction relates would also have been an offence in the United Kingdom if it had been done there at the time of the defendant's conviction for the current offence. *Paragraph 9* amends section 270B of the Armed Forces Act 2006. Section 270B provides for the award of a community punishment where an offender, guilty of an offence, has on three or more previous occasions been convicted and sentenced to a fine only. The amendment provides for previous convictions by a court in another European Union member State to be taken into account to the same extent as previous convictions in the United Kingdom, provided that the offence to which the conviction relates would also have been an offence in the United Kingdom if it had been done there at the time of the defendant's conviction for the current offence.

Required custodial sentences for certain offences
642.   Section 110 of the Powers of Criminal Courts (Sentencing) Act 2000 (the 2000 Act) provides for a minimum sentence of seven years' imprisonment where a person aged 18 or over at the time of the offence is convicted of a third class A drug trafficking offence in England and Wales, unless the court considers it would be unjust to do so in all the circumstances of the case. A class A drug trafficking offence may be committed anywhere in the UK. Section 111 of that Act similarly provides for a minimum sentence of three years' imprisonment where a person aged 18 or over at the time of the offence is convicted of a third domestic burglary in England and Wales. Only previous domestic burglaries committed in England and Wales are counted. Section 113 of that Act provides that certificates of conviction which are in accordance with the requirements of that section are evidence of convictions in relation to a class A drug trafficking offence or a domestic burglary.

643.   *Paragraph 10* extends section 110 of the 2000 Act to require a previous conviction by a court in another European Union member State to be taken into account to the same extent as a previous conviction in the UK, provided that the offence to which the conviction relates would have constituted a class A drug trafficking offence if it were done in the UK at the time of the conviction. Only offences committed after the time that the amendment comes into force will be relevant.

644.   Section 111 of the 2000 Act is extended so that a previous conviction by a court in another European Union member State, or a conviction by a court in another part of the UK, must be taken into account to the same extent as a previous domestic burglary conviction in England and Wales, provided that the offence to which the conviction relates would have constituted domestic burglary if it were done in England and Wales at the time of the conviction. Only offences committed after the time that the amendment comes into force will be relevant.

645.   Also amended is section 113 of the 2000 Act, to make provision for the treatment of certificates of convictions produced by courts in other parts of the UK outside England and Wales and in European Union member States.

Restriction on imposing custodial sentence or service detention
646.   *Paragraph 11* amends section 263 of the Armed Forces Act 2006, which imposes a restriction on imposing a custodial sentence or service detention on an unrepresented offender. The restriction does not apply if the offender was aged 21 or over when convicted, and has previously been sentenced to imprisonment by a civilian court in the UK, or for a service offence. Section 263 is amended to include a previous sentence to detention by a court in any other European Union member State.

Young offenders: referral conditions
647.   *Paragraph 12* of Schedule 15 makes changes to the conditions which must be satisfied for a young offender to be sentenced to a referral order by amending section 17 of the 2000 Act to take account of convictions obtained in another European Union member State.

648.   When a child or young person is given a referral order, he or she is required to attend a youth offender panel, which is made up of two volunteers from the local community and a panel adviser from a youth offending team. The panel, with the young person, their parents/carers and the victim (where appropriate), agree a contract lasting between three and 12 months. The aim of the contract is the prevention of reoffending by the offender.

649.   Section 17 of the 2000 Act has been amended by section 35 of the 2008 Act and, although these changes have not yet come into force, references below are to the 2000 Act as amended.

650. Section 17(1) of the 2000 Act sets out the conditions which, if met, require the court to make a referral order ("the compulsory referral conditions"). They apply where a young offender aged under 18 appears before a UK court, has no previous convictions and pleads guilty to the offence or offences with which they are charged. Paragraph 12(2) extends the provision in respect of what count as previous convictions, so that a previous conviction by a court in another European Union member State will count in the same way as a conviction by a UK court, so that a young offender with previous convictions in another European Union member State will fall within the compulsory referral conditions.

651. Section 17(2A) to (2C) of the 2000 Act set out the circumstances in which a court may, but is not obliged to, impose a referral order ("the discretionary referral conditions"). Where the compulsory referral conditions are not satisfied, a referral order may be made where the young offender pleads guilty to the offence or at least one of the other offences they are charged with and the young offender:

a) has not been convicted previously in a UK court;

b) has been convicted only once before in a UK court and has not previously received a referral order, or

c) has been convicted more than once before a UK court and received a referral order on only one other occasion (subject to further conditions).

652. Paragraph 12(3) to (5) make amendments to these conditions so that convictions by or before a court in another European Union member State are treated in the same way as a conviction by or before a UK court (making allowance for the fact that of course an offender convicted in another European Union member State cannot have received a referral order in respect of that conviction).

Proving of foreign convictions before courts
653. Section 73 of the Police and Criminal Evidence Act 1984 enables convictions (or acquittals) for offences in the UK to be proved by means of a certificate of conviction (or acquittal) signed by the proper officer of the court. At present, overseas convictions are proved under section 7 of the Evidence Act 1851, which requires that the judgment either be sealed by the foreign court or signed by the judge of the foreign court. *Paragraph 13* of Schedule 15 amends section 73 of the Police and Criminal Evidence Act 1984 so as to extend the procedures for proving convictions or acquittals in other member States of the European Union by way of certificates signed by the proper officer of the court.

654. Section 74 of the Police and Criminal Evidence Act 1984 provides that the fact that a person other than the accused has been convicted of an offence by a UK court, or a service court, is admissible in evidence for the purpose of proving that that person committed the offence. It also provides that where a person other than the accused is proved to have been convicted of an offence by or before a UK court or a service court, he or she must be taken to have committed that offence unless the contrary is proved; and it establishes a presumption that any person convicted of an offence in the UK actually committed it. *Paragraph 14*

amends section 74 so that convictions for offences in other European Union member States are treated in the same way as UK convictions.

655.   Section 75 of the Police and Criminal Evidence Act 1984 makes certain documents, such as the charge-sheet, admissible as evidence of the facts on which a conviction was based for the purposes of section 74. It also provides that a copy of a document which is purported to be certified or authenticated by or on behalf of the court or authority having custody of that document, where the document is admissible under this section, is to be taken to be a true copy of that document unless the contrary is proved. *Paragraph 15* amends section 75 to extend these provisions to documents relating to convictions in other European Union member States.

656.   Sections 73 to 75 of the Police and Criminal Evidence Act 1984 extend to England and Wales only. Equivalent provision to sections 73 to 75 is made for Northern Ireland in the Police and Criminal Evidence (Northern Ireland) Order 1989.

657.   *Paragraphs 16 to 18* make similar amendments to the 1989 Order as are provided by *paragraphs 13 to 15* for the 1984 Act.

Section 145: Transfer to Parole Board of functions under the Criminal Justice Act 1991
658.   Section 145 applies the same early release arrangements to all long-term prisoners sentenced under the Criminal Justice Act 1991 whose release at the half-way point of sentence remains a matter for Parole Board discretion. It amends section 35(1) of the Criminal Justice Act 1991 (power to release long-term prisoners) so that after a long-term prisoner has served half his or her sentence a recommendation by the Parole Board to release him or her is binding on the Secretary of State.

659.   The section also inserts a new section 37(5A) into the Criminal Justice Act 1991, which provides that, where a prisoner is released at the discretion of the Parole Board under section 35(1), the Secretary of State may only set, vary or cancel licence conditions in accordance with the Board's recommendations.

Section 146: Retention of knives surrendered or seized: England and Wales
660.   Sections 54 to 56 of the Courts Act 2003 set out grounds for the surrender, seizure and retention of certain articles carried by persons entering court buildings. In particular, section 55 provides, with certain exceptions, that seized or surrendered items must be returned when the owner leaves the court building.

661.   *Subsection (3)* of section 146 inserts a new section 55A, into the Courts Act 2003, to provide a different procedure for the retention of all knives that have been surrendered to, or seized by, a court security officer. New section 55A(2) provides that section 55 does not apply where a knife is seized by or surrendered to a court security officer. Under new section 55A, knives must be retained, unless returned or disposed of in accordance with regulations under section 55A(5) or 56.

662. New section 55A(4) provides that, if the court security officer reasonably believes that a retained knife may be evidence of, or in relation to, an offence, he or she can retain the knife for so long as necessary to enable the court security officer to draw it to the attention of a police constable.

663. Under new section 55A(5), the Lord Chancellor must make provision in regulations, subject to the negative resolution procedure, for the procedure to be followed when a knife is retained, the making of requests for the return of retained knives and the procedure for the return of knives. Under section 56, regulations can make provision about the disposal of unclaimed knives.

664. New section 55A(6) states that the definition of a knife includes "a knife-blade and any other article which (a) has a blade or is sharply pointed, and (b) is made or adapted for use for causing injury to the person".

Section 147: Retention of knives surrendered or seized: Northern Ireland
665. Section 147 provides a similar scheme for Northern Ireland by amending paragraph 5 of, and adding a new paragraph 5A into, Schedule 3 to the Justice (Northern Ireland) Act 2004.

Section 148: Security in tribunal buildings
666. Section 148 provides for Part 4 of the Courts Act 2003 to be applied in respect of tribunal buildings as it does for courts. Part 4 of the Courts Act 2003 details the powers of court security officers and the circumstances in which they may exercise them lawfully. It also sets out grounds for the surrender, seizure and retention of certain articles carried by persons entering court buildings.

667. *Subsection (1)* gives the Lord Chancellor power, by order subject to the affirmative resolution procedure, to provide for the designation of security officers in tribunal buildings. The order may apply the provisions in Part 4 of the Courts Act 2003 with any necessary modifications. Part 4 includes the powers in new section 55A of that Act (inserted by section 146) which provides different procedure for the retention of all knives that have been surrendered to or seized by a court security officer. Under the new section 55A of the Courts Act 2003 knives must be retained, unless returned or disposed of in accordance with regulations under sections 55A(5) or 56.

668. The definition of "tribunal buildings" and other definitions are set out in *subsection (3)*. "Tribunal buildings" includes buildings used by the following tribunals: the First-tier Tribunal, the Upper Tribunal, employment tribunals, the Employment Appeal Tribunal, and the Asylum and Immigration Tribunal. Subsection (3) also gives the Lord Chancellor power to designate by order further tribunals whose buildings are to be included in the definition of "tribunal buildings". This section extends to England and Wales only; therefore the provision of security arrangements under section 148 can only apply to UK-wide tribunals listed in section 39(1) of the Tribunals, Courts and Enforcement Act 2007 (the 2007 Act) when they are sitting in England and Wales.

Part 6 - Legal aid and other payments for legal services

Section 149: Community Legal Service: pilot schemes

669.   The creation of the Community Legal Service (CLS) was part of the Government's fundamental reform of the legal aid system, as set out in the Access to Justice Act 1999.

670.   The purpose of the CLS is to ensure that individuals who qualify financially and have reasonable grounds for bringing or being part of any action, can receive publicly funded legal assistance in civil matters that are within scope of the civil scheme.

671.   The Legal Services Commission (LSC) was created under the Access to Justice Act 1999, and has responsibility for administering the CLS Fund, and setting priorities about the types of services that may be funded; or for carrying out any changes to funding priorities that the Lord Chancellor directs are necessary.

672.   The services that may be funded through the CLS Fund are set out in the Funding Code, which also sets out the criteria according to which the LSC decides whether or not to fund services.

673.   As the LSC continuously monitors, reviews and enhances the services being provided through the CLS, it will occasionally need to explore or pilot new ways of delivering specialist services so that the costs and benefits can be judged in practice. Section 18A of the Access to Justice Act 1999 (inserted by section 58 of the 2008 Act) contains a power to pilot schemes in relation to the Criminal Defence Service (CDS), but at present there is no express power to pilot civil schemes under the CLS within the Act.

674.   Section 149 amends the Access to Justice Act 1999 to give express power to pilot schemes as part of the CLS. Section 6(8) of the Access to Justice Act 1999 empowers the Lord Chancellor to direct or authorise the LSC to fund the provision of particular types of legal services in specified circumstances. *Subsection (2)* of the section inserts new subsections (8A) and (8B) into section 6 of the 1999 Act to make it clear that the circumstances specified in a direction or authorisation may relate to particular areas or courts and that a direction or authorisation may require or authorise the LSC to fund the provision of certain types of legal service only for particular classes or selections of people.

675.   *Subsection (3)* inserts a new section 8A into the Access to Justice Act 1999. New section 8A will enable the Funding Code to contain provisions ("pilot provisions") which are to have effect for period not exceeding three years. The pilot provisions of the Funding Code will be capable of having a limited application; for example the pilot provisions may apply only in relation to a particular area specified in the Code or only in relation to particular classes of person specified in the Code. At the end of the three-year pilot period the LSC will be able to decide whether to amend the Funding Code so that the pilot provisions have a more general application.

676. *Subsection (4)* makes a consequential amendment to section 9(5) of the Access to Justice Act 1999. The effect of the amendment is that a revised version of the Funding Code which contains changes made in pursuance of new section 8A will not come into force until it has been approved by a resolution of both Houses of Parliament.

677. *Subsection (5)* inserts a new section 11A into the Access to Justice Act 1999. The effect of new section 11A is that subordinate legislation made under the 1999 Act in relation to the CLS will be capable of having a limited application. For example, it will be possible to make subordinate legislation in relation to the CLS that applies only in relation to a particular area or only in relation to a particular description of court. New section 11A specifies that the length of subordinate legislation made in pursuance of the new section is limited to three years. The Lord Chancellor may extend this period to cover any gap between the end of the pilot and extending the pilot more generally.

678. *Subsection (6)* amends section 25 of the Access to Justice Act 1999 to provide for the parliamentary procedure for delegated legislation containing pilot schemes.

Section 150: Excluded services: help in connection with business matters
679. Schedule 2 to the Access to Justice Act 1999 lists those legal services which may not be funded as part of the CLS.

680. Paragraph 1(h) of Schedule 2 currently excludes services consisting of the provision of help in relation to matters arising out of the carrying on of a business. Business cases were excluded from the scope of civil funding as they are low priority cases and alternative forms of funding are available. In addition, only individuals may make applications or be funded as part of the CLS.

681. *Subsection (2)* of section 150 omits paragraph 1(h) and *subsection (3)* replaces it with a new paragraph 1A. The new paragraph clarifies that as well as cases arising out of the carrying on of a business, which can be any activity carried out by an individual with a view to profit, cases which relate to an individual planning or proposing to set up a business, or cases which relate to the transfer or termination of a business, are also excluded from the CLS. Examples are disputes that arise out of the carrying on of a business that is no longer trading and disputes arising out of the preliminary steps of establishing a business regardless of whether the business exists at the time of the application.

Section 151: Criminal Defence Service: information requests
682. This section amends section 17A of and Schedule 3 to the Access to Justice Act 1999. *Subsection (1)* extends the power to seek information from the Commissioners for Her Majesty's Revenue and Customs (HMRC) and the Secretary of State, which at present may be exercised for purposes relating to an individual's financial eligibility for legal aid services, to cover purposes relating to an individual's liability to make contributions towards the cost of those services.

683.   *Subsections (3) to (5)* amend paragraph 6 of Schedule 3 to the Access to Justice Act 1999 to provide that requests may be made for information relating to a time specified in the request, as well as for information as at the date of the request. *Subsection (7)* is a consequential amendment to paragraph 7 of Schedule 3 (restrictions on disclosure).

684.   *Subsection (4)* amends paragraph 6 of Schedule 3 to allow requests to be made for any previous names or addresses of an individual and for information about an individual's benefit status at any time specified in the request.

685.   *Subsection (5)* amends paragraph 6 of Schedule 3 to allow requests to the Commissioners to be made for information about whether or not an individual is (or at any time was) self-employed and for information about an individual's benefit status at any time.

686.   *Subsection (6)* amends paragraph 6 of Schedule 3 to allow information requests to be made about an individual's assets as well as income.

687.   *Subsection (8)* amends paragraph 8 of Schedule 3 to clarify how requests as to an individual's employment apply where the individual is an office-holder, and to delete an unnecessary provision relating to the 1998 Act.

Section 152 and Schedule 18: Criminal Defence Service: enforcement of order to pay cost of representation
688.   Section 152 amends sections 17 and 17A of the Access to Justice Act 1999. It also introduces Schedule 18 which inserts new Schedule 3A into that Act.

689.   *Subsection (2)* inserts new subsection (4) and (5) into section 17 of the Access to Justice Act 1999 to set out particular matters that may be provided for by regulations on the enforcement of recovery of defence costs orders.

690.   Such regulations may provide for the addition of the costs of enforcing liability under a recovery of defence costs order to the amount which is unpaid and, for this purpose new subsection (5) adds a definition of "overdue sum".

691.   Under new subsection (4) regulations will be able to provide that overdue sums are recoverable summarily as a civil debt, that is to say through magistrates' courts in accordance with the Magistrates' Courts Act 1980. The regulations will also be able to provide that overdue sums are recoverable, if a county court or the High Court so orders on the application of the person owed the sums, as if they were payable under an order of that court in accordance with rule 70.5 of the Civil Procedure Rules (The Civil Procedure (Amendment No 3) Rules 2008, SI 2008/3327), thereby making it unnecessary to begin fresh proceedings in respect of the debt.

692.   *Subsection (3)* inserts new subsections (2A) to (2E) into section 17A of the Access to Justice Act 1999. New subsection (2A) provides, as for recovery of defence costs orders, that enforcement regulations may add the costs of enforcing liability under a contribution order to the amount which is unpaid, and in addition that any overdue sums are recoverable summarily as a civil debt or recoverable, if a county court or the High Court so orders, as if they were payable under an order of that court. Enforcement regulations may also provide for the withdrawal of an individual's right to representation in certain circumstances and may empower courts to make motor vehicle orders. These are defined in new subsection (2B) of section 17A as clamping orders and vehicle sale orders, which are themselves defined in new subsections (2C) and (2D) of section 17A. Under a vehicle sale order a motor vehicle which has been fitted with an immobilization device in accordance with enforcement regulations may be sold and the proceeds of sale applied in paying the overdue sum. *Subsection (4)* inserts new Schedule 3A to the Access to Justice Act 1999.

693.   New Schedule 3A sets out further provisions relating to motor vehicle orders. Paragraph 2 of new Schedule 3A states that enforcement regulations may in particular make provision for the procedure for making an order, what matters must be included in the order, the fitting of clamping devices and notices to motor vehicles, the removal and storage of motor vehicles, the release of the clamp or the motor vehicle from storage, the conditions which need to be met before the release, sale or other disposal of an unreleased motor vehicle, the imposition of charges in connection with any of the above and the recovery of such charges.

694.   Paragraph 3 of new Schedule 3A requires enforcement regulations to provide that a motor vehicle order may be made only on the application of the person or body to which the overdue sum is owed (in practice this is likely to be the LSC).

695.   Before a clamping order is made the court must be satisfied (paragraph 4 of new Schedule 3A) that the person has wilfully refused or culpably neglected to pay and that the value of the motor vehicle, if sold, would be likely to be an amount which exceeds half of the estimated recoverable amount. The estimated recoverable amount is the combined total of the amount of the overdue sum and the amount of charges likely to be due under the enforcement regulations.

696.   Enforcement regulations must also provide (paragraph 5 of new Schedule 3A) that a clamping order may be made only in relation to a vehicle which is owned by the individual liable to pay the overdue sum. A clamping order may not be made in relation to a vehicle used by a disabled person (paragraph 6 of new Schedule 3A).

697.   Paragraph 7 of new Schedule 3A provides that enforcement regulations must also state that no vehicle sale order may be made in respect of the vehicle before the end of a specified period.

Section 153: Statutory instruments relating to the Legal Services Commission

698. Part 1 of the Access to Justice Act 1999 contains a number of powers for the Lord Chancellor to make orders or regulations in respect of the services provided by the LSC as part of the CLS or CDS. However, that Act does not currently contain a general power, which is commonly found in primary legislation, for such secondary legislation to include consequential, incidental, supplementary, transitional, transitory or saving provision.

699. *Subsection (3)* inserts a new subsection (8A) into section 25 of the Access to Justice Act 1999 so that secondary legislation made by the Lord Chancellor (whether in relation to the CLS or the CDS) may include consequential, incidental, supplementary, transitional, transitory and saving provisions.

700. *Subsection (2)* is a consequential amendment to section 2 of the Access to Justice Act 1999 (power to replace LSC with two bodies). Section 2(2) of that Act is no longer needed as the effect of that subsection is replicated by new subsection 25(8A).

Section 154: Damages-based agreements relating to employment matters

701. Section 154 provides for the regulation of damages-based agreements in respect of claims relating to employment matters. It does this by inserting a new section 58AA into the Courts and Legal Services Act 1990. Damages-based agreements cannot be used in court proceedings but are commonly used by solicitors and claims managers in cases before an employment tribunal.

702. Subsection (1) of the new section 58AA provides that damages-based agreements relating to employment matters which satisfy certain conditions are not unenforceable by reason only of being damages-based agreements. Those damages-based agreements relating to employment matters which do not satisfy the prescribed conditions are unenforceable by virtue of subsection (2).

703. Subsection (3) defines a "damages-based agreement" as an agreement between a person providing advocacy services, litigation services or claims management services and the recipient of those services. The amount that the recipient pays for those services is determined by reference to the amount recovered by him or her from the claim or from proceedings before an employment tribunal.

704. Subsection (4) sets out the conditions that damages-based agreements relating to employment matters must satisfy in order to be enforceable. Subsection (5) enables the Lord Chancellor to make regulations (by affirmative resolution procedure) under subsection (4) and allows different provision to be made in respect of different descriptions of agreements.

705. Subsection (6) sets out the persons who must be consulted before regulations are made. As with regulations made under section 58 of the Courts and Legal Services Act 1990 which regulates conditional fee agreements, this includes senior judiciary, those representing the legal profession and others as the Lord Chancellor considers appropriate. Subsection (7) defines the terms "payment" and "claims management services" for the purposes of the new section 58AA.

Part 7 - Criminal Memoirs etc

Section 155: Exploitation proceeds orders
706.   *Subsection (1)* provides the High Court (or the Court of Session in Scotland) with the power to make an exploitation proceeds order. This is an order made in relation to a qualifying offender who has obtained exploitation proceeds from a relevant offence. The effect of an order is to require the offender (called the "respondent") to pay a sum of money to the enforcement authority in respect of those proceeds.

707.   *Subsection (3)* explains that a person obtains exploitation proceeds from a relevant offence if he or she derives a benefit from the exploitation of any material relating to the offence or any steps taken with a view to such exploitation. So, for example, a person who receives payment for writing a book, or giving a television interview, about their crime will have obtained exploitation proceeds. A person will also have derived a benefit if he or she receives a payment but the book is not published or the interview does not go ahead.

708.   *Subsection (4)* explains that an order must specify a recoverable amount and identify the benefits derived by respondent to which the order relates. *Subsection (6)* provides that if the respondent does not pay the recoverable amount by the required time he or she must pay interest at the appropriate rate for the period that the amount is unpaid. The appropriate interest rate is defined in *subsection (8)* as that specified in section 17 of the Judgments Act 1838 or, in the case of an order made in Scotland, the rate payable under a decree of the Court of Session.

Section 156: Qualifying offenders
709.   An exploitation proceeds order can only be made in respect of a person who is a qualifying offender and this section sets out who is a "qualifying offender" for the purposes of the provisions. A person is a qualifying offender if they have been convicted of an offence in a United Kingdom court, have been found not guilty by such a court by reason of insanity or have been found by such a court to be suffering from a disability and to have done the act charged (*subsection (2)*). In addition, under *subsection (3)* a United Kingdom national, resident or person resident in the United Kingdom at the time of an offence will be a qualifying offender if they have been convicted by a court outside the United Kingdom of a foreign offence or if that court makes a finding equivalent to a finding that the person was not guilty by reason of insanity or equivalent to a finding that the person was under a disability and did the act charged. *Subsection (4)*, in conjunction with *subsection (6)*, defines a foreign offence as an act or omission, amounting to an offence under the law in force in the foreign country that, at the time it was committed, would have been an offence if committed in the United Kingdom and which would be an offence if done in the United Kingdom at the time that the application for an exploitation proceeds order is made.

Section 157: Qualifying offenders: service offences
710.   This section makes supplementary provision to section 156 in respect of service offences under UK and foreign service law.

Section 158: Qualifying offenders: supplementary

711.   This section ensures that the Rehabilitation of Offenders Act 1974 does not prevent account being taken of a conviction for the purposes of this Part, and makes equivalent provision for Northern Ireland. It also disapplies provisions which provide that an offence is not treated as a conviction where an offender is given an absolute or conditional discharge in respect of it.

Section 159: Relevant offences

712.   This section sets out what is a "relevant offence" for the purposes of section 155. A relevant offence is a serious offence committed by a person as a result of which that person falls within the definition of a qualifying offender, a serious offence taken into consideration by a court when sentencing a person for the offence which results in the person being a qualifying offender, or a serious offence committed by a third party which is associated with the offence which results in a person being a qualifying offender (or it is associated with an offence which is taken into consideration by the court when sentencing a person for an offence which results in the person being a qualifying offender). *Subsections (3) and (4)* set out when an offence will amount to an "associated offence". Offences are associated with each other if they are committed in the context of the same joint criminal venture or if one of the offences is on the list of offences at subsection (4).

713.   Subsection (2) defines a "serious" offence as one that is triable only on indictment or, in the case of a foreign offence, an offence that would be so triable had it been committed in the United Kingdom at the time that the application for the order is made. Subsections (6) and (7) make equivalent provision in relation to UK and foreign service offences.

Section 160: Deriving a benefit

714.   This section sets out what amounts to "deriving a benefit" for the purposes of section 155. *Subsection (2)* explains what amounts to "exploitation" and provides that exploitation can be by any means including publishing material in written or electronic form, using any media from which visual images, words or sounds can be produced and live entertainment, representation or interview.

715.   *Subsection (3)* provides that the offender will be deemed to have derived a benefit if he or she secures the benefit for himself or herself or secures the benefit for another person. This ensures that a qualifying offender cannot circumvent the scheme by arranging for exploitation proceeds to be paid directly to a third party.

716.   The effect of *subsection (4)* is that it is irrelevant whether the benefit is derived, or the exploitation takes place, in the United Kingdom or before or after conviction for the relevant offence. This would be relevant, for example, where an offender is paid for the story of his crime while he was standing trial and is subsequently convicted. However, where the relevant offence is an offence committed by a third party, the respondent must have committed the associated offence before deriving the benefit.

717.   *Subsection (5)(a)* ensures that the scheme does not apply retrospectively. The scheme applies to offences whenever committed, but benefits derived before the provisions are commenced will not be recoverable under the new scheme.

Section 161: Applications

718.	This section provides that the court may only make an exploitation proceeds order on the application of an enforcement authority. *Subsection (2)* explains that the enforcement authority in relation to England and Wales and Northern Ireland is the Serious Organised Crime Agency or a person prescribed by order made by the Secretary of State. The Scottish Ministers are the enforcement authority for Scotland.

719.	*Subsection (3)* provides that an enforcement authority in England and Wales may only apply for an exploitation proceeds order with the consent of the Attorney General. An enforcement authority in Northern Ireland may apply for such an order only with the consent of the Advocate General for Northern Ireland (which, under paragraph 45 of Schedule 22 is to be read as a reference to the Attorney General for Northern Ireland until the relevant sections of the Justice (Northern Ireland) Act 2002 come into force).

Section 162: Determination of applications

720.	This section sets out a range of factors that the court must take into consideration when deciding whether to make exploitation proceeds order in respect of any benefit and, if it makes an order, the recoverable amount to be specified in the order. *Subsection (3)* lists the specific matters that the court must take into account but the list is not exhaustive and the court may take into account any other matters it considers relevant.

Section 163: Limits on recoverable amount

721.	This section places a limit on the amount that the court can order a person to pay (known as the "recoverable amount"). The "recoverable amount" cannot exceed the total value of the benefits derived by the offender (including those secured for a third party) in respect of which the order is made. The order must identify the benefits it relates to. Also the recoverable amount cannot exceed the funds available to the offender (the "available amount"). *Subsection (2)* also provides that the recoverable amount may be a nominal amount.

722.	*Subsection (3)* provides that the order may include benefits derived by the offender up until the time the court makes its determination. But it cannot seek to include benefits that have already been subject to a previous order.

723.	Where the offender receives a benefit in kind rather than cash, *subsections (4) and (5)* set out how the value of the benefit is determined. Subsection (4) provides that where the benefit is a benefit in kind rather than cash the value of the benefit is the market value at the time the benefit is received minus anything that the respondent (or in the case of a benefit secured for a third person, that person) paid for it. If a particular benefit has no market value, subsection (5) provides that the court can attribute to the benefit such value as is just and reasonable.

724.   There may be circumstances where an offender receives payment from a publisher, but only a small part of the payment directly relates to material pertaining to a relevant offence. This could arise, for example, where a criminal is paid to write a series of magazine articles about his life, but only one article in the series relates to the relevant offence. *Subsection (6)* gives the court the discretion to decide what proportion of the benefit it is just and reasonable to attribute to the exploitation of material pertaining to the relevant offence.

Section 164: The available amount
725.   This section defines the "available amount". This is the sum which, if lower than the total value of the benefits from exploitation included in the order, will be the maximum that a respondent can be ordered to pay. The available amount is the total value of the respondent's assets, any benefits secured by the respondent for a third party (for example where the respondent has asked the publisher to pay proceeds from a book to a family member) and the value of any relevant gifts that the court considers it just and reasonable to take into account. *Subsection (2)* defines the value of the respondent's assets as the value of all the free property held by the respondent, less the total amount payable in respect of obligations that have priority. *Subsection (3)* sets out that property is free unless it is subject to certain types of forfeiture, deprivation and other types of orders. *Subsection (4)* defines priority obligations. Such obligations will include court fines and liabilities such as mortgages. A relevant gift is defined in *subsection (6)* as a gift made on or after the time the respondent derived any of the benefits identified in the order. A gift includes transaction at a significant undervalue.

Section 165: Property
726.   This section defines the meaning of property for the purposes of section 164.

Section 166: Effect of conviction being quashed
727.   This section addresses the situation where the court has made an exploitation proceeds order and a conviction relevant to the order is quashed. The effect of *subsection (1)(a)* is that, where the relevant offence is within section 159(1)(a) (a serious offence that results in the respondent being a qualifying offender) and the conviction for that offence is quashed, the order ceases to have effect. The effect of *subsection (1)(b)* is that, where the relevant offence is within section 159(1)(b) (a serious offence taken into consideration by a court when determining the sentence for an offence that results in the respondent being a qualifying offender) or section 159(1)(c) (a serious offence committed by a third person associated with the offence that results in the respondent being a qualifying offender or taken into consideration when determining the sentence for such an offence) and the respondent's conviction or convictions that result in the relevant offence being within section 159(1)(b) or (c) is (or are) quashed, the order ceases to have effect. If the order is made in respect of more than one offence and subsections (1)(a) or (b) applies in relation to each, the order ceases to have effect. On an application by the respondent, the court must order the Secretary of State (in Scotland, the Scottish Ministers) to repay to the respondent the sum that the respondent paid to satisfy the order (excluding any amount paid in respect of interest for late payment), known as "the recovered amount", together with interest at a rate to be determined by the court. *Subsection (4)* addresses the situation where one, but not all, such convictions are quashed or where an associated conviction mentioned in section 159(1)(c) is quashed. In such cases, on application by the respondent, the court has the discretion to decide that the order should cease to have effect; to reduce the recoverable amount by such amount as it considers

is just and reasonable; or to leave the order in place without alteration. If the court determines that the order should cease to have effect, the court must order the Secretary of State to repay the recovered amount together with interest at a rate to be determined by the court. If the court decides to reduce the recoverable amount and the offender has already paid a sum in excess of the new amount, the court must order the Secretary of State to repay the difference (with interest at a rate to be determined by the court).

Section 167: Powers of court on repeat applications

728.   This section confers on the court certain powers where an application for an exploitation proceeds order is made in relation to a person and the court has previously made an exploitation proceeds order in respect of that person. This may arise, for example, where an offender publishes a new edition of the autobiography that led to the original order being imposed and receives a further payment for the new edition. Under this section, the court can adopt any finding of fact made by the court in connection with the earlier order. If both orders relate to benefits derived from the same source, the court must also have regard to its previous determination of the recoverable amount specified in the earlier order.

Section 168: Additional proceeds reporting orders

729.   This section provides that a court making an exploitation proceeds order can also make an additional proceeds reporting order if it believes that the likelihood of the respondent obtaining further exploitation proceeds is so high as to justify making such as order. An additional proceeds reporting order works in the same way as a financial reporting order in sections 76 to 81 of the 2005 Act. The effect is that a person subject to such an order is required to report on specified particulars of his or her financial affairs at specified periods. The period for such an order must not exceed 20 years. This type of order might be considered appropriate, for example, where a publisher has agreed to pay the offender in instalments or where royalties from a particular publication flow into the offender's account over a lengthy period.

Section 169 and Schedule 19: Exploitation proceeds investigations

730.   Section 168 and Schedule 19 amend Part 8 of POCA so as to extend the provisions relating to investigations to include exploitation proceeds investigations. This means, for example, that the enforcement authority carrying out an exploitation proceeds investigation is able to apply to a judge for a production order or search and seizure warrant.

Section 170: Functions of Serious Organised Crime Agency

731.   This section makes consequential changes to the functions of the Serious Organised Crime Agency.

Section 171: Limitation

732.   *Subsection (1)* inserts a new section 27C into the Limitation Act 1980. *Subsections (1) to (3)* have the effect that an application for an exploitation proceeds order may not be made more than six years after the enforcement authority's cause of action accrued. *Subsection (4)* provides that a cause of action will accrue from the time that the enforcement authority has actual knowledge that a person has obtained exploitation proceeds from a relevant offence.

733.   *Subsection (2)* inserts new section 72C into the Limitation (Northern Ireland) Order (SI 1989/1339) which makes similar provision for Northern Ireland.

734.   Subsection (3) inserts a new section 19C into the Prescription and Limitation (Scotland) Act 1973. This makes similar provision for Scotland, although in that case the limitation period is five rather than six years, in line with other provision made by that Act.

Section 172: Interpretation of Part 7
735.   This section sets out the meaning of terms used in this Part of the Act.

Part 8 - Data Protection Act 1998

Section 173: Assessment notices
736.   Section 173 inserts new sections 41A, 41B and 41C into the 1998 Act. New section 41A(1) enables the Information Commissioner to carry out an assessment to determine whether a data controller has complied or is complying with the data protection principles. The Information Commissioner is not required to seek the consent of the data controller to undertake this assessment. Under this subsection, the Information Commissioner will be able to issue an assessment notice, which will require the subject of the notice to take certain action as set out in section 41A(3).

737.   New section 41A(2) provides that the data controllers that may be served with an assessment notice are government departments, public authorities designated for the purposes of section 41A by an order made by the Secretary of State and other persons of a description so designated.

738.   New section 41A(3) lists the requirements that may be included in an assessment notice. These include permitting the Commissioner to enter any specified premises and observe the processing of any personal data that takes place on the premises. The recipient of an assessment notice may be required to direct the Commissioner to any documents, equipment or other material on the premises that are of a specified description and to assist the Commissioner to view any information of a specified description that is capable of being viewed using equipment on the premises. The recipient of the notice may be required to permit the Commissioner to inspect or examine any of the documents, information, equipment or material to which the Commissioner is directed or which the Commissioner is assisted to view. The recipient may also be required to comply with any request from the Commissioner for a copy of any of the documents to which the Commissioner is directed and a copy (in a form requested by the Commissioner) of any of the information which the Commissioner is assisted to view. Finally, the notice may require the recipient to make available for interview by the Commissioner persons who process personal data on behalf of the data controller (and are willing to be interviewed).

739.   New section 41A(5) sets out that the assessment notice must specify either the time when, or the period within which, the requirements of the notice must be complied with.

740.   New section 41A(6) sets out that assessment notices must contain particulars of the rights of appeal conferred by section 48 of the 1998 Act.

741.   New section 41A(7) provides that the Commissioner may cancel an assessment notice. This is to be done by giving a written notice to the data controller on whom the assessment notice was served.

742.   New sections 41A(8) and 41A(11) oblige the Secretary of State to consider, at least every five years, whether it is still appropriate for a public authority, and necessary for a description of data controller, to be designated by order and, therefore, be subject to assessment notices.

743.   New section 41A(9) provides that the Secretary of State must not designate a description of data controller as liable for assessment notices without a recommendation from the Information Commissioner. It also provides that before making an order to designate a description of data controller, the Secretary of State must consult such persons as appear to the Secretary of State to represent the interests of persons of the description to be designated and such other persons as the Secretary of State considers appropriate.

744.   New section 41A(10) sets out the test that must be applied by the Information Commissioner when deciding whether to make a recommendation, and the Secretary of State when deciding whether to make an order to designate a description of data controller. They must be satisfied that designation is necessary having regard to the nature and quantity of data under the control of such persons, and any damage or distress which may be caused by a contravention by such persons of the data protection principles.

745.   New section 41A(12) provides two definitions. It provides a definition of "public authority", for the purpose of the order-making power in section 41A(2)(b), as any body, office-holder or other person in respect of which an order may be made under section 4 or 5 of the Freedom of Information Act 2000 or under section 4 or 5 of the Freedom of Information (Scotland) Act 2002. This adds to and expands the definition of public authority in section 1(1) of the 1998 Act, which provides that public authority means a public authority as defined by the Freedom of Information Act 2000 or a Scottish public authority as defined by the Freedom of Information (Scotland) Act 2002.

746.   Section 41B(1) provides that the time or period given for compliance with an assessment notice must allow time for an appeal to be brought under section 48 of the 1998 Act. The result of this is that the need to comply with an assessment notice will be suspended if an appeal is brought.

747.   New section 41B(2) establishes an exception to section 41B(1) by virtue of which, if there are special circumstances, the Commissioner can ask the data controller to comply with a requirement in an assessment notice as a matter of urgency. In this case the notice can take effect after seven days, beginning with the day on which the assessment noticed is served. The assessment notice in this case will need to include a statement that the Commissioner

considers that the notice must be complied with as a matter of urgency and the Commissioner's reasons for that conclusion.

748.   New section 41B(3) ensures protection for material benefiting from legal professional privilege. An assessment notice does not have effect in relation to material that meets one of the tests set out in this subsection.

749.   New section 41B(5) provides a number of exclusions from the powers to give assessment notices. They do not apply to a judge, which is defined in section 41C(6) as including a justice of the peace (or, in Northen Ireland, a lay magistrate), a member of a tribunal, and a clerk or other officer entitled to exercise the jurisdiction of a court or tribunal. In this section, tribunal means any tribunal in which legal proceedings may be brought.

750.   Bodies specified in section 23(3) of the Freedom of Information Act 2000 are also excluded under section 41A(5). Those bodies are:

- the Security Service,

- the Secret Intelligence Service,

- the Government Communications Headquarters,

- the special forces,

- the Tribunal established under section 65 of the Regulation of Investigatory Powers Act 2000,

- the Tribunal established under section 7 of the Interception of Communications Act 1985,

- the Tribunal established under section 5 of the Security Service Act 1989,

- the Tribunal established under section 9 of the Intelligence Services Act 1994,

- the Security Vetting Appeals Panel,

- the Security Commission,

- the National Criminal Intelligence Service,

- the Service Authority for the National Criminal Intelligence Service, and

- the Serious Organised Crime Agency.

751.   Finally, the Office for Standards in Education, Children's Services and Skills, is excluded from the scope of assessment notices, but only in so far as it is a data controller in respect of information processed for the purposes of functions exercisable by Her Majesty's Chief Inspector of Education, Children's Services and Skills by virtue of section 5(1)(a) of the Care Standards Act 2000.

752.   New section 41C of the 1998 Act requires the Information Commissioner to produce a code of practice in relation to the exercise of his or her new function of issuing assessment notices. Section 41C(1) requires the Commissioner to produce the code and section 41C(2) provides a non-exhaustive list of the matters that must be covered by the code.   Section 41C(3) provides that the code must make provision about access to health information and social care information. Section 41C(4) deals with the content of the report produced by the Commissioner as a result of an assessment notice. Section 41C(5) and (6) provide that the Commissioner may alter or replace the code and that such a replacement or altered code must be issued by the Commissioner. Section 41B(7) provides that any code must be approved by the Secretary of State before being issued.   Section 41B(8) requires the Commissioner to publish the code.

Section 174: Data-sharing code of practice
753.   This section inserts new sections 52A to 52E into the 1998 Act. New section 52A places the Information Commissioner under a duty to publish and keep under review a data-sharing code of practice.

754.   New section 52A(1) and (2) provide that the code will contain practical guidance and any other guidance that promotes good practice in the sharing of personal data. Good practice is defined as practice that appears to the Information Commissioner to be desirable including, but not limited to, compliance with the requirements of the 1998 Act. When deciding what constitutes good practice, the Information Commissioner must have regard to the interests of data subjects and others.

755.   New section 52A(3) requires that in preparing the code the Information Commissioner must consult, as he or she considers appropriate, with trade associations, data subjects and persons who represent the interests of data subjects.

756.   New section 52A(4) defines sharing of personal data as the disclosure of the data by transmission, dissemination or otherwise making it available. For example the sending of files, the granting of access to a database and the publication of information all amount to "sharing" under this definition.

757.   New section 52B(1) requires that once the Information Commissioner has prepared the code it must be submitted to the Secretary of State for approval.

758.   New section 52B(2) provide that approval may be withheld only if the Secretary of State is of the opinion that the code is incompatible with any community obligations (such as EC Directive 95/46/EC on the protections of individuals with regard to the processing of personal data and on the free movement of such data) or any international obligations of the UK (such as the Convention for the protection of individuals with regard to automatic processing of personal data: Convention 108 of the Council of Europe).

759.   If approval is withheld, new section 52B(3) requires the Secretary of State to publish the reasons for this. If approval is granted, the Secretary of State must lay the code before Parliament.

760.   New section 52B(4) to (11) makes provision relating to the issuing of the code. In particular, either House of Parliament has 40 days (excluding any period during which Parliament is not sitting for more than four days) in which to pass a resolution refusing to approve the code. If such a resolution is passed, or if the Secretary of State withholds approval, then the Information Commissioner is obliged to prepare another code of practice for approval. Where approval is granted and no resolution is passed, the Information Commissioner must issue the code. The code then comes into force 21 days later.

761.   New section 52C(1) requires the Information Commissioner to keep the code under review and empowers him or her to prepare an alteration or replacement to the code. New Section 52C(2) obliges the Information Commissioner to alter or replace the code if he or she becomes aware that application of the code could give rise to a claim that the UK was in any way in breach of its European Community or other International obligations.

762.   New section 52C(3) requires the Commissioner in preparing an alteration or replacement code to consult, as he or she considers appropriate, with trade associations, data subjects and such persons who represent the interests of data subjects. New section 52C(4) provides that section 52B (with the exception of subsection (6)) applies equally to a replacement code or an alteration to the code.

763.   New section 52D makes provision for the code, any replacement code and any alteration, to be published by the Information Commissioner.

764.   New section 52E provides that although the code cannot of itself give rise to legal proceedings, a person's breach or compliance with the code is to be taken into account by the courts, the Information Tribunal, and the Commissioner, whenever it is relevant to a question arising in legal proceedings or in connection with the exercise of the Commissioner's functions. So, for example, the Information Commissioner is entitled to consider levels of compliance with the data-sharing code of practice when evaluating whether to instigate enforcement action in relation to an instance of data-sharing. Equally a court would be entitled to have regard to levels of compliance with the code where it was attempting to resolve an issue relating to whether or not a particular person had fulfilled their legal obligations by complying with good practice.

Section 175 and Schedule 20: Further amendments of the Data Protection Act 1998

765.   This section introduces Schedule 20, which makes amendments to the 1998 Act.

Data Controllers' Registration

766.   *Paragraph 1* of Schedule 20 amends section 16(1) of the 1998 Act. The Information Commissioner is obliged under section 19 of the 1998 Act to maintain a register of data controller notifications. Section 17(1) of the 1998 Act prohibits the processing of personal data unless the data controller has an entry recording his or her details in the register of data controllers. Section 18(5) of the 1998 Act provides that where a data controller notifies the Information Commissioner, the notification must be accompanied by such fee as may be prescribed by fees regulations. Under section 19(2) of the 1998 Act each register entry shall consist of the registrable particulars of the data controller and such other information as is required by the notification regulations. The term "registrable particulars" is defined in section 16(1). The amendment in paragraph 1 adds a new registrable particular to section 16(1) of the 1998 Act (new subparagraph (h)).

767.   The new registrable particular is such information about the data controller as is prescribed under new section 18(5A) of the 1998 Act. Section 18(5A) is inserted by *paragraph 2* of Schedule 20 and provides that notification regulations may prescribe the information about the data controller that is required for the purpose of verifying the fee payable under section 18(5). If false information is provided in a notification then this may be an offence under section 5 of the Perjury Act 1911, Article 10 of the Perjury (Northern Ireland) Order 1979 (SI 1979/1714 (NI 19)) or section 44(2) of the Criminal Law (Consolidation) (Scotland) Act 1995.

768.   *Paragraph 3* of Schedule 20 amends section 19 of the 1998 Act to add a new subsection (8). It provides that the Information Commissioner will not be required to comply with section 19(6) and (7) in relation to the information that has to be supplied under new section 16(1)(h). Section 19(6) provides for the Information Commissioner to make the register of notifications available to the public for inspection and available to the public in such other ways as he or she considers appropriate. Section 19(7) requires the Information Commissioner to provide certified copies of registrable particulars in the register of notifications to members of the public.

769.   *Paragraph 4* amends section 20 of the Act to enable regulations to be made requiring data controllers to notify the Information Commissioner of any changes to their registrable particulars for the purpose of ensuring that the correct annual notification fee is paid. Data controllers will not need to provide the Information Commissioner with this information year after year whenever they pay their notification fee. Instead, they will need to provide this information only upon a change of circumstance. Any failure to comply with a duty imposed by such regulations may be an offence under section 21(2) of the 1998 Act.

770.   The overall effect of these amendments is to provide a way for the Information Commissioner to check that a data controller has paid the correct notification fee.

Assessment notices

771.   *Paragraphs 5 and 6* of Schedule 20 make three amendments that are consequential on the creation of new sections 41A and 41B of the 1998 Act by section 173. *Paragraph 5* amends section 48 of the 1998 Act to provide a right of appeal to the tribunal against an assessment notice.   Paragraph 6 amends section 67 of the 1998 Act to specify the parliamentary procedure that is to be followed by the Secretary of State in making orders under the power in new section 41A(2)(b) (power to designate specific public authorities as being within the scope of Assessment Notices) and 41A(2)(c) (power to designate a person of a description as being within the scope of Assessment Notices). Such orders will be subject to the negative resolution procedure and the affirmative resolution procedure respectively. *Paragraph 7* inserts a new definition of government department into section 70(1) of the 1998 Act.

Power to require information

772.   *Paragraph 8* of Schedule 20 amends section 43 of the 1998 Act to strengthen the Information Commissioner's powers for inspecting a data controller's compliance with the data protection principles, using an information notice.

773.   *Paragraph 8*(3) inserts two new subsections into section 43 of the 1998 Act, which contains the power of the Information Commissioner to issue an information notice. New section 43(1A) allows an information notice to require that the data controller must provide (a) particular information as specified; (b) information of a particular description; or (c) information in a category as specified or described. New section 43(1B) allows an information notice to require that the information is provided (a) within a specified period; (b) at a specified time and place; (c) in a specified form.

774.   *Paragraph 9* provides an equivalent amendment (to that made in paragraph 8 detailed above) to section 44 of the 1998 Act for special information notices (which makes special provisions in relation to the processing of personal data for journalistic, artistic and literary purposes).

Restriction on the use of information

775.   *Paragraph 10* of Schedule 20 amends section 43 of the 1998 Act to place restrictions on the use of certain information obtained under the newly extended information notice power.

776.   Paragraph 10(3) inserts three new subsections into section 43 of the 1998 Act. These subsections make provision to ensure that the principle against self-incrimination is protected in relation to this section. First, the new section prohibits a data controller from being required to provide information which would incriminate him or her in relation to proceedings other than proceedings for offences under the 1998 Act, and certain perjury offences. Second, statements made under the new expanded power of section 43 cannot be used as evidence against the data controller for any data protection offence (other than the offence of failing to comply with the terms of an information notice), unless the accused acts in such a way as to forfeit this particular protection. In those circumstances evidence of the original statement would be admissible in order to rebut the false assertions made by the accused.

777.   *Paragraph 11* of Schedule 20 provides for an equivalent amendment to that made in paragraph 10 to be made to section 44 of the 1998 Act relating to special information notices (which makes special provisions in relation to the processing of personal data for journalistic, artistic and literary purposes).

778.   *Paragraph 12* of Schedule 20 amends paragraph 11 of Schedule 7 to the 1998 Act to make provision in relation to the principle against self-incrimination. This existing provision of the 1998 Act provides that data controllers are not obliged to satisfy subject access requests under section 7 of the 1998 Act, where to do so would reveal incriminating evidence of an offence other than an offence under the 1998 Act.   The amendment adjusts the provisions so that neither the 1998 Act offences nor certain perjury offences are covered by this protection.

Monetary penalties: restriction on matters to be taken into account
779.   Section 55A of the 1998 Act provides for the Information Commissioner to issue a monetary penalty for serious breaches of the data protection principles of a kind likely to cause substantial damage or distress that are carried out either deliberately or recklessly.

780.   Under section 51(7) of the 1998 Act the Information Commissioner can, with the consent of the data controller, assess any processing of personal data for the following of good practice.

781.   *Paragraph 13* of Schedule 20 amends section 55A of the 1998 Act to prevent the imposition of a monetary penalty based on information that has been obtained from a good practice assessment (section 51 of the 1998 Act) or the use of an assessment notice under new section 41A of the 1998 Act as inserted by section 173.

Warrant for entry and inspection
782.   *Paragraph 14* of Schedule 20 amends Schedule 9 to the 1998 Act to give broader inspection powers to the Information Commissioner in relation to warrants obtained under Schedule 9 to the 1998 Act.

783.   Paragraph 14(2) amends paragraph 1 of Schedule 9 to give a circuit judge or a District Judge (Magistrates' Courts) the power to grant a warrant to the Information Commissioner on the grounds that a data controller has failed to comply with the requirements of an assessment notice.

784.   Paragraph 14(3) broadens the range of activities the Information Commissioner can engage in when executing a warrant granted under Schedule 9. In particular, it gives the Information Commissioner the power to require any person on the premises to provide an explanation of any document or other material found on the premises (new paragraph 1(3)(e)) and to require such a person to provide information that is reasonably required to determine whether there has been any contravention of the data protection principles (new paragraph 1(3)(f)).

785.   Paragraph 14(4) and 14(5) provide for amendments to Schedule 9 to the 1998 Act that are consequential on the introduction of warrants for failure to comply with an assessment notice. Under the amendments in paragraph 14(4) the requirement in paragraph 2(1)(a) of Schedule 9 to the Data Protection Act 1998, that before a warrant can be issued the Information Commissioner must give seven days' notice in writing to the data controller demanding access to the premises, cannot be satisfied by serving a data controller with an assessment notice. The amendment in paragraph 14(5) reflects the fact that the new test for granting a warrant would not be dependent on the Information Commissioner finding evidence on the premises to be searched.

786.   Paragraph 14(6) makes amendments to paragraph 12 of Schedule 9 to the 1998 Act, which provides a criminal offence for the obstruction of, or failure to assist, a person executing a warrant under that Schedule. The additional text extends the offence to cover deliberately or recklessly making false statements in response to the new powers to require information created in paragraph 14(3) detailed above.

787.   Paragraph 14(7) provides protection against self-incrimination for any person required to provide information under the extended powers created under paragraph 14(3) above. In particular, any information provided by that person in response to these new powers under a warrant cannot be used as evidence in criminal proceedings against that person. However, this protection is not absolute, and the response given can be used in evidence if the offence concerned is either the offence of obstructing or failing to assist a person executing a Schedule 9 warrant or is one of a specific group of perjury offences. Furthermore the response can be used in evidence for the prosecution of any criminal offence if the accused acts in such a way as to forfeit this particular protection. In those circumstances evidence of the original statement becomes admissible in order to rebut the false assertions made by the accused.

Part 9 - General

Section 176: Orders, regulations and rules
788.   This section makes provision in connection with the various powers under the Act to make orders, regulations and rules. The affirmative resolution procedure applies to statutory instruments made under the powers listed in *subsection (5)*. The effect of *subsection (4)* is that all other powers are subject to the negative resolution procedure or, in the case of the power to make commencement orders, no procedure applies. *Subsection (3)* provides that any power under the Act to make orders, regulations or rules includes a power to make provision generally or only for specified purposes, cases, circumstances or areas and to make different provision for different purposes, cases, circumstances or areas. This subsection also enables orders and regulations to make incidental, supplementary, consequential, transitional, transitory or saving provisions.

Section 177 and Schedules 21 and 22: Consequential etc. amendments and transitional and saving provisions

789.   This section enables the Secretary of State by order to make supplementary, incidental, consequential, transitory, transitional or saving provision for the purposes of the Act. It is a power to make consequential provisions for those purposes at any time, including amendments to primary and secondary legislation. The section also introduces Schedule 21 (minor and consequential amendments) and Schedule 22 (transitory, transitional and saving provisions).

Schedule 21: Minor and consequential amendments
Part 1 - Coroners
790.   The 1953 Act is amended by *paragraphs 6 to 21* of Schedule 21. Paragraphs 8(3)(e), (4) and (5) and 9(3)(c) and (d) and (4) change the time within which an informant is required to provide information for the registration of a death. Time begins to run from the date of confirmation by the medical examiner of the cause of death by virtue of section 18 of the Act or at the date of discontinuation of a coroner's investigation under section 4 of the Act, rather than at the date of death. *Paragraphs 8 and 9* also extend the categories of those who have a duty to give information for the registration of a death to include the partner of the deceased and the deceased's personal representative. These terms are defined in the same way as in the list of interested persons given in section 47.

791.   *Paragraph 13* of Schedule 21 omits section 21 of the 1953 Act so that the Registrar General no longer needs to authorise the registration of a death where this is requested more than 12 months after the death. This provision is removed because all deaths will be reviewed either by a coroner or medical examiner under the provisions of Part 1 of the Act.

792.   *Paragraph 14* of Schedule 21 substitutes a new section 22 of the 1953 Act so as to remove the provisions for issuing medical certificates of cause of death. The provisions are replaced by powers in section 20 for the Secretary of State to make regulations for the certification of cause of death. Section 22 of the 1953 Act is also amended to require the registrar to record the cause of death where this is provided under regulations made under section 20. References to section 22 elsewhere in the 1953 Act are amended to refer to regulations under section 20.

793.   *Paragraph 18* of Schedule 21 amends section 29 of the 1953 Act so that an error of fact or substance in the cause of death recorded in an entry in a death register may not be corrected without the approval of the appropriate medical examiner or senior coroner where the recorded cause had been confirmed under section 20 or on discontinuance of an investigation under section 4 (following post-mortem).

794.   *Paragraph 19* inserts a section 33A into the 1953 Act, creating an entitlement to obtain (on payment of a fee) a short certificate of death. The inserted section is based on section 33 of the 1953 Act (short certificate of birth).

795.   The majority of the remaining amendments relating to Part 1 pick up references to the term "inquest" in other legislation and replace these with references to "investigation" or pick up references to the 1988 Act and replace these with references to the provisions of the Act.

796.   The 1996 Act is amended by *paragraphs 37 to 42* of Schedule 21. Northern Ireland is subject to the 1996 Act and this will not change with the reforms; treasure and treasure trove cases will continue to be investigated by the local coroners in Northern Ireland.   The amendments to the Treasure Act in relation to England and Wales are therefore disapplied for Northern Ireland (*paragraphs 38, 39(5)* and *41*).

797.   Under the amendment made by *paragraph 40* the Secretary of State will be able to make an order, using the negative resolution procedure, which will designate specified officers to receive reports of treasure from finders, acquirers or any other person.   The designated officer will then pass the information on to the Coroner for Treasure.

798.   Paragraph 40 also amends the 1996 Act so as to increase the period for prosecuting a person for not reporting an item believed to be treasure by a finder to the Coroner for Treasure from six months to a maximum of three years.   This period of prosecution will also apply to a breach of the duty to report on acquirers.

799.   There is an amendment to the Human Tissue Act 2004 relating to coroners' duties in respect of bodies prior to transplantation or other similar or related activities at paragraphs 47 to 50.

Part 2 – Murder and Suicide
800.   Paragraph 52 of Schedule 21 amends Schedule 21 to the Criminal Justice Act 2003 (determination of minimum term in relation to mandatory life sentence) consequential upon abolishing the partial defence to murder of provocation and replacing it with a new partial defence set out in section 54 (partial defence to murder: loss of control.

Part 9 - Disqualification for Driving
801.   Sections 34 and 35 of the Road Traffic Offenders Act 1988 provide that where an offender has more than one previous disqualification for a period of 56 days or more a higher minimum period of disqualification applies.   Sections 34A to 34C of the Road Traffic Offenders Act 1988 provide for a reduction in the period of disqualification for offenders convicted of drink-driving offences who successfully complete an approved driver retraining course.   Similarly, sections 34D to 34G and 41B of the Road Traffic Offenders Act 1988, when implemented, will provide for an offender convicted of a "relevant drink offence" to obtain a reduced period of disqualification for that offence by agreeing to participate, at his or her own expense, in an alcohol ignition interlock programme.   Section 35 of the Road Traffic Offenders Act 1988 determines the minimum period of disqualification for a repeat offender. Section 37 of that Act deals with the effect of the disqualification in terms of when the licence is revoked and comes back into effect, including disregarding any period of suspension pending an appeal.   Section 42 provides for an application to be made to the court for the removal of disqualification after a certain period has expired.   Section 47 requires courts to send to the Secretary of State for endorsement licences of persons disqualified for 56 days or more.

802.   *Paragraph 90* of Schedule 21 provides for an extension period generated by provisions inserted by Schedule 16 (that is, section 35A or 35B of the Road Traffic Offenders Act 1988, section 248D of the Criminal Procedure (Scotland) Act 1995, or section 147A of the Powers of Criminal Courts (Sentencing) Act 2000) to be disregarded in certain circumstances. These are as follows: when a court is determining whether an offender's previous driving disqualifications included more than one previous disqualification for a period of 56 days or more, such as to attract a higher minimum period of disqualification; in calculating any appropriate reduction in the length of the disqualification; the minimum period of disqualification; the time before an application can be made for removal of a disqualification under the Road Traffic Offenders Act 1988; and determining whether the length of the ban is less, or more, than 56 days, as appropriate.

803.   *Paragraph 91* makes similar amendments to the Road Traffic Offenders (Northern Ireland) Order 1996 about disregarding an extension period arising because of Article 8A of the Criminal Justice (Northern Ireland) Order 1980, Article 40A of the Road Traffic Offenders (Northern Ireland) Order 1996 or Article 91A of the Criminal Justice (Northern Ireland) Order 2008.

804.   Section 54 of the Crime (International Co-operation) Act 2003 gives effect to mutual recognition of disqualification for driving so that drivers normally resident in one member State of the European Union who are disqualified from driving in another member State will also be disqualified in their state of residence. *Paragraph 93* of Schedule 21 inserts a new subsection, subsection (3A), into that section so that an extension period is disregarded for the purposes of the minimum period of disqualification which requires notification to a central authority.

Part 10 - Miscellaneous

805.   *Paragraph 94* of Schedule 21 amends section 160 of the 2000 Act. It substitutes subsection (2) of section 160 effectively repealing parts of it. But, where the Secretary of State makes an order under section 107(1)(e) specifying the types of accommodation that may be "youth detention accommodation", this order will still be subject to the negative resolution procedure. This paragraph also substitutes subsection (5) of section 160 to provide that an order under section 107(1)(e) may make different provision for different cases or classes of case.

806.   *Paragraph 98* of Schedule 21 makes minor amendments to the Criminal Justice and Immigration Act 2008. Amongst other things, the amendments change the date that a youth rehabilitation order comes into effect to the day that it is made, unless the court specifies a later date.

Schedule 22: Transitory, transitional and saving provisions

807.   Under *paragraph 1* of Schedule 22, the Lord Chancellor must make an order so that all existing coroners' districts will become coroner areas and will be known by the name by which the coroner's district was previously known (but ending coroner area rather than coroner's district). *Paragraph 2* of Schedule 22 provides that the relevant authority for each new coroner area will be the authority which had been the relevant council for the coroner's district from which it was derived.

808.   *Paragraph 3* provides that any person who was a coroner for a district immediately before the 1988 Act was repealed will be treated as having been appointed as a senior coroner under paragraph 1 of Schedule 3 for the corresponding coroner area. It also provides that any person who was a deputy coroner or assistant deputy coroner under the 1988 Act will be treated as having been appointed as an assistant coroner under paragraph 2(4) of Schedule 3 for the corresponding coroner area.

809.   *Paragraph 3* also enables a solely medically qualified coroner, or coroner over 70, who was appointed under the 1988 Act, to continue to be a coroner if for example their own jurisdiction merges with a neighbouring one following implementation of the Act. This provision will enable the small number of coroners, who are medically rather than legally qualified and/or over 70, and who will be treated as appointed on implementation of the Act, to become coroners/assistant coroners if their areas are altered by an order under Schedule 2.

810.   *Paragraphs 14 to 21* make detailed transitional provision in relation to investigation anonymity orders and witness anonymity orders. This is required, primarily, for two reasons. First, the replacement by the Armed Forces Act 2006 of earlier arrangements for service courts and, secondly, the replacement by Part 3, Chapter 2, of the original witness anonymity order provisions in the CEWAA. The transitional provisions deal, for example, with the situation where a witness anonymity order has been made under the CEWAA and which requires discharge or variation after the present Act comes into force. This includes orders made by old style service courts in cases where the new service courts under the Armed Forces Act 2006 will in future exercise jurisdiction.

811.   *Paragraph 46* provides a transitional provision in relation to the reference to District Judge (Magistrates' Courts) in new paragraph 1(1A) of Schedule 9 to the 1998 Act, as inserted by paragraph 14(2) of Schedule 20 (new powers for the Information Commissioner to apply for a warrant for failure to comply with the requirements of an assessment notice). The effect of the transitional provision is that new paragraph 1(1A) is to be read as if the words "District Judge (Magistrates' Courts)" were omitted until paragraph 8 of Schedule 4 to the Courts Act 2003 is commenced.

Section 178 and Schedule 23: Repeals
812.   This section introduces Schedule 23. That Schedule repeals existing legislative provisions which have been replaced by provisions in the Act or otherwise are no longer required. In particular, it repeals the whole of the 1988 Act.

Section 180:   Effect of amendments to provisions applied for the purposes of service law.
813.   This section provides that where criminal justice provisions are applied for the purposes of service law, they are to apply as amended by this Act.

Section 181: Extent
814.   This section sets out the extent of the provisions of the Act. Details are in paragraphs 53 to 58 above.

Section 182: Commencement

815. This section provides for commencement. Details are in paragraphs 816 to 819 below.

COMMENCEMENT

816. The following provisions of the Act come into force on Royal Assent:

- Sections 47 and 48, which contain the interpretation provisions for Part 1 of the Act and the transitional provisions in Part 1 of Schedule 22;

- Section 116 (and associated transitional provision and repeal) which removes the requirement for bills of indictment to be signed;

- Section 143 (and associated minor amendment in paragraph 96 of Schedule 21 and repeal) which relates to the implementation of the E-Commerce and Services Directives;

- Sections 151 and 152 and Schedule 18 which make provision in respect of criminal legal aid;

- Section 154 which makes provision in respect of damages-based agreements in relation to employment matters;

- In Part 9, sections 176, 177(3) to (10), 179, 181 to 183; and

- Paragraphs 62(3) and 92 to 95 of Schedule 21 (and associated repeals) which contain minor drafting corrections.

817. The following provisions of the Act will come into force two months after Royal Assent:

- Section 73 (and the related minor and consequential amendments and repeals in Part 4 of Schedule 21 and Part 2 of Schedule 23) which abolishes the common law offences of sedition, seditious libel, defamatory libel and obscene libel in England and Wales and Northern Ireland;

- Section 138 (and associated transitional provision in paragraph 38 of Schedule 22) which adds certain terrorism offences to the list of offences in respect of which a public protection sentence may be passed in England and Wales.

818.   Chapter 2 of Part 3, which repeals and re-enacts the provisions of the CEWAA, comes into force on 1 January 2010. (By virtue of section 14 of the CEWAA no new witness anonymity orders may be made under that Act after 31 December 2009.) The associated minor and consequential amendments in paragraphs 67 to 69 of Schedule 21, the associated transitional provisions in paragraphs 17 to 23 of Schedule 22 and associated repeals in Part 3 of Schedule 23 also come into force on 1 January 2010.

819.   All other provisions will be brought in force by means of commencement orders.

HANSARD REFERENCES

820.   The following table sets out the dates and Hansard references for each stage of the Act's passage through Parliament.

Stage	Date	Hansard reference
House of Commons		
Introduction	14 January 2009	Vol 486 Col 230
Second Reading	26 January 2009	Vol 487 Col 26-125
Committee	3 February 2009 5 February 2009 10 February 2009 24 February 2009 26 February 2009 3 March 2009 5 March 2009 10 March 2009	Hansard Public Bill Committee Coroners and Justice Bill
Report Report and Third Reading	23 March 2009 24 March 2009	Vol 490 Col 52-140 Vol 490 Col 188-274
House of Lords		
Introduction	25 March 2009	Vol 709 Col 660
Second Reading	18 May 2009	Vol 710 Col 1204-1302
Committee	9 June 2009 10 June 2009 23 June 2009 30 June 2009 7 July 2009 9 July 2009 13 July 2009 15 July 2009 21 July 2009	Vol 711 Col 558-628 Vol 711 Col 682-734 Vol 711 Col 1463-1570 Vol 712 Col 119-214 Vol 712 Col 569-664 Vol 712 Col 790-866 Vol 712 Col 941-1036 Vol 712 Col 1184-1260 Vol 712 Col 1526-1580

These notes refer to the Coroners and Justice Act 2009 (c.25)
which received Royal Assent on 12 November 2009

Report	21 October 2009	Vol 713 Col 709-802
	26 October 2009	Vol 713 Col 981-1094
	28 October 2009	Vol 713 Col 1169-1263
	29 October 2009	Vol 713 Col 1278-1316
Third Reading	5 November 2009	Vol 714 Col 380-426
Consideration of Amendments		
Commons consideration of Lords amendments	9 November 2009	Vol 499 Col 51-130
Lords consideration of Commons reasons and amendments	11 November 2009	Vol 714 Col 823-872
Commons consideration of Lords reasons and amendments	12 November 2009	Vol 499 Col 370-388

Royal Assent – 12 November 2009   House of Commons Hansard Vol 499 Col 418
House of Lords Hansard   Vol 714 Col 918

ANNEX A

GLOSSARY

1933 Act	Administration of Justice (Miscellaneous Provisions) Act 1933
1953 Act	The Births and Deaths Registration Act 1953
1957 Act	Homicide Act 1957
1959 Act	Coroners (Northern Ireland) Act 1959
1976 Act	Fatal Accidents and Sudden Deaths Inquiry (Scotland) Act 1976
1984 Rules	Coroners Rules 1984
1988 Act	Coroners Act 1988
1996 Act	Treasure Act 1996
1998 Act	Data Protection Act 1998
1999 Act	Youth Justice and Criminal Evidence Act 1999
2000 Act	Powers of Criminal Courts (Sentencing) Act 2000
2001 Act	International Criminal Court Act 2001
2003 Act	Criminal Justice Act 2003
2005 Act	Serious Organised Crime and Police Act 2005
2007 Act	Tribunals, Courts and Enforcement Act 2007
2008 Act	Criminal Justice and Immigration Act

	2008
BBFC	British Board of Film Classification
BIS	Department for Business, Innovation and Skills
CDS	Criminal Defence Service
CLS	Community Legal Service
CASC	Constitutional Affairs Select Committee
CEWAA	Criminal Evidence (Witness Anonymity) Act 2008
DMACC	Deputy Medical Adviser to the Chief Coroner
ECHR	European Convention on Human Rights
E-Commerce Directive	Directive 2000/31/EC on certain legal aspects of information society services, in particular electronic commerce, in the Internal Market
FSA	Financial Services Authority
HMRC	Her Majesty's Revenue and Customs
HRA	Human Rights Act 1998
ISS	Information society services
LHB	Local Health Board
LSC	Legal Services Commission
MACC	Medical Adviser to the Chief Coroner
MCCD	Medical Certificate of Cause of Death
MRI	Magnetic Resonance Imaging

*These notes refer to the Coroners and Justice Act 2009 (c.25)
which received Royal Assent on 12 November 2009*

NME	National Medical Examiner
PCT	Primary Care Trust
POCA	Proceeds of Crime Act 2002
SAP	Sentencing Advisory Panel
SGC	Sentencing Guidelines Council
Services Directive	Directive 2006/123/EC on Services in the Internal Market

Printed in the UK by The Stationery Office Limited under the authority and superintendence of Carol Tullo, Controller of Her Majesty's Stationery Office and Queen's Printer of Acts of Parliament

12/2009   440206   19585